CASE STUDIES IN EDUCATION AND CULTURE

General Editors

GEORGE *and* LOUISE SPINDLER
Stanford University

EDUCATION IN REBHAUSEN

A German Village

EDUCATION IN REBHAUSEN

A German Village

RICHARD L. WARREN
Stanford University

HOLT, RINEHART AND WINSTON
New York • Chicago • San Francisco • Toronto • London

To Ethel, Deborah, and Dick

Foreword

About the Series

This series of case studies in education and culture is designed to bring to students in professional education and in the social sciences the results of direct observation and participation in educational process in a variety of cultural settings. Individual studies will include some devoted to single classrooms, others will focus on single schools, some on large communities and their schools; still others will report on indigenous cultural transmission where there are no schools at all in the Western sense. Every attempt will be made to move beyond the formalistic treatments of educational process to the interaction between the people engaged in educative events, their thinking and feeling, and the content of the educational process in which they are engaged. Each study will be basically descriptive in character but since all of them are about education they are also problem-oriented. Interpretive generalizations are produced inductively. Some are stated explicitly by the authors of the studies. Others are generated in the reader's mind as hypotheses about education and its environmental relationships.

The cross-cultural emphasis of the series is particularly significant. Education is a cultural process. Each new member of a society or a group must learn to act appropriately as a member and contribute to its maintenance and, occasionally, to its improvement. Education, in every cultural setting, is an instrument for survival. It is also an instrument for adaptation and change. To understand education we must study it as it is—imbedded in the culture of which it is an integral part and which it serves.

When education is studied this way, the generalizations about the relationship between schools and communities, educational and social systems, education and cultural setting that are current in modern educational discussions, become meaningful. This series is, therefore, intended for use in courses in comparative and overseas education, social foundations and the sociology of education, international educational development, culture and personality, social psychology, cultural dynamics and cultural transmission, comparative sociology—wherever the interdependency of education and culture, and education and society, is particularly relevant.

We hope these studies will be useful as resources for comparative analyses, and for stimulating thinking and discussion about education that is not confined by one's own cultural experience. Without this exercise of a comparative, transcultural perspective it seems unlikely that we can acquire a clear view of our own educational experience, or view education in other cultural settings without ethnocentric bias.

About the Author

Richard L. Warren is a research associate at the Stanford Center for Research and Development in Teaching. He holds a doctoral in the social foundations of education from Stanford University, with concentrations in history and anthropology. While at Stanford he was an instructor in social foundations. He completed his undergraduate work at Harvard University in 1947 and received an M.A. from Peabody College for Teachers in 1949. From 1947 to 1949 he served in the Education Division of the Office of Military Government for Bavaria in Germany, and from 1952 to 1962 he taught history at Indian Springs School, Helena, Alabama.

About the Book

This case study of education in a German village is in the tradition of anthropological studies of small communities. School and village are seen not as interdependent but separate entities, but as interrelated dimensions of a distinctive way of life. Dr. Warren and his family participated in this way of life in Rebhausen, a community of about 3000 persons, for a year.

The study is particularly significant because Rebhausen, like most traditional communities the world over, is subject to the impact of rapid industrialization and urbanization. Everywhere this impact is disruptive of the established culture and its maintenance. In Germany the distinctive variations in dialect, religion, and local custom that have traditionally characterized rural areas are giving away, often rapidly and painfully, sometimes more slowly, to the urban way of life. The school of the traditional rural German community has operated to maintain and reinforce cultural patterns molded by time to the local ecology and social system. But now the validity of these functions is being challenged. And yet in Rebhausen the traditional relationships of the school and community exert strong influence on the behavior of teachers, parents, officials, and students. The village school still functions as a stabilizing institution reflecting and transmitting the traditional village culture. Pressure for innovation originates largely from outside the school program, from the state, and in some degree from the children. The dilemma is that in order to maintain an effective role in German society (or any other society) the school must adapt to, if not lead, sociocultural change, but in its present form the school in Rebhausen, and in similar communities, is a symbol of and in fact a major contributor to cultural stability. Can this school maintain continuity with the past and at the same time adapt to radical change?

George and Louise Spindler
General Editors
STANFORD 1966

Preface

The fieldwork on which this book is based was conducted in 1964–1965 under a grant from the United States Office of Education, Cooperative Research Program. Supplementary aid came through a fellowship granted by Stanford University and the Deutscher Akademischer Austauschdienst.

The point of view about education which the book reflects owes much to the influence of George D. Spindler, and I am deeply indebted to him for his counsel in the development and implementation of the research. Richard E. Gross, Kurt Steiner, and Hans N. Weiler read an earlier version of the manuscript and made valuable recommendations. I wish to thank Hans N. Weiler for his aid in locating a site in southwest Germany and in establishing contacts with local officials.

Fictitious names have been used for the village, its residents, and surrounding communities. In the course of the research I was privileged to enjoy the acquaintance of many individuals who will remain unidentified but whose assistance was invaluable. I especially wish to express appreciation for the reaction of Rebhausen residents. Their friendliness and openness made the study possible.

Limitations of space preclude a more thorough treatment of the community itself. Much has been written about Germans, their character, political habits, family life, and social institutions. The events of the past three decades compound the implications and possible interpretations which can be attached to research on German life. I wish to emphasize that this is a study of only one German elementary school in one German village.

R.L.W.

Palo Alto, California
December 1966

ix

Contents

Introduction

THIS IS a study of the role of the school in a rural German village, which is undergoing rapid cultural change as a result of industrialization. The school, in this study, is regarded as a transmitter of the community culture and as a potential mediator of cultural change rather than simply as an academic institution. The study, therefore, is concerned with both the formal, systematic aspects of the educational process and the more informal, noncurricular, and even nonintended aspects.

The study was conducted in Rebhausen, a community of 3400 located at the edge of the Engelskrone, a hilly section in southwest Germany. In the selection of a site, primary consideration was given to locating a village which traditionally had been rural and isolated but which was beginning to experience directly and rather abruptly the impact of industrialization and urbanization. Rebhausen was especially appropriate as a site because a chemical plant had been established there in 1958, with a work force which had grown in six years from less than 100 to over 900.

In the fall of 1964 my wife and I and our two children established residence in Rebhausen. The German schools were already in session; we enrolled our daughter, age fourteen, in a Waldstadt Gymnasium and our son, age twelve, in the Rebhausen elementary school. I began the study with systematic observations in the Rebhausen school, spending about a week in each grade. During the remainder of the year I revisited certain grades as time allowed. The school was a good point of departure. It was central to the study and afforded an opportunity to begin establishing contacts with a variety of individuals, particularly parents. The principal and teachers were friendly and cooperative, making available curricular materials and relevant statistics—and above all finding the time to talk about the problems and demands of teaching in Rebhausen.

During the early months of the study I also attended innumerable public gatherings. The mayor overlooked few opportunities to help me become better acquainted with life in the village, at least the more formal organizational aspects. He invited me to meetings which concerned him directly and made arrangements for my attendance at other meetings. In practically all cases I was introduced and my purpose for being in Rebhausen briefly explained.

Observations in the school and attendance at public meetings provided contacts which led in many cases to lengthy informal conversations and formal interviews. To achieve a more systematic and representative account of village life I arranged

1

interviews with individuals representing different age groups, vocational pursuits, periods of residence, and particular social and organizational interests. Extended interviews were conducted with over forty individuals; the time spent with any one person ranged from three hours to over twenty-five hours.

The results of this study will be presented in that order which will best clarify the role of the school as a stabilizing, mediating institution in the midst of change. Change in the life of the community is personified by the native of Rebhausen who was once a full-time farmer but is now a factory worker and part-time farmer. Shift work in the factory and the mechanization of farm operations have created for him a different rhythm of life, affecting and changing the time he invests in the traditional community institutions. The factory itself has brought to village life an urban-oriented population of newcomers from all over Germany. This new social presence constitutes a basic force for change. In order to clarify, therefore, the role of the school in the midst of change, it is necessary first to discuss farming and the factory, the two basic elements of tradition and change. Around and in these primary economic institutions cluster activities, patterns of social interaction, attitudes and values—the ingredients of tradition and change in the village. This will be followed by chapters on the school, with particular attention to a reconstruction of the enculturation process and to relationships with basic institutions inside and outside the community. The stabilizing role of the school will be assessed according to the extent to which school life mirrors the traditional life of the community. The mediating role of the school will be assessed according to those elements in the school program which are directed at preparing students for a dynamic, urban-technological society.

1 / The community: tradition and change

EVERY APPROACH to Rebhausen offers landscapes rich in the natural beauty of southwest Germany. Traveling northwest from Waldstadt one can easily locate the hilly region to which Rebhausen belongs. The two roads leading out of Waldstadt traverse through several small villages onto a plain, checkered with small, intensely cultivated fields. The roads wind through the fields and along creeks, offering restful, pastoral scenes so common to this part of Germany.

But these two roads do not provide the same, immediate impressions of the village. We made frequent trips to Waldstadt, and our return route usually depended on mood as much as convenience, since the distances are about the same. Approaching the northeast corner of the village we could dwell on its historic, rural isolation and on the lush, hovering presence of the wine tradition. From this corner the village is barely visible; only the red-orange tiled roofs loom above the fruit trees which mask the buildings themselves. Directly behind the village, almost above it, rise the terraced vineyards, an uneven pattern of small plots asserting in their totality a kind of legitimate domination over the village.

The introduction from the southeast corner is to a different Rebhausen, contemporary but disharmonious. The industrial complex is located here. The unimaginative, rectangular buildings of the factory itself and of the housing development clutter the landscape and disrupt the natural beauty of the vineyards.

The approach from the west, high above Rebhausen, suggests the agrarian character of the village life and the natural beauty of the region. The road follows the valley and the small undulating hills of the Engelskrone and then rises through a pass opening down to Rebhausen. From the pass the upper Rhine plain and the mountains beyond Waldstadt merge into a scene which dwarfs the village and conveys the ascendancy of the natural surroundings. For a stranger the scene is impressive; for a student of the village life it is also significant. A constant renewal of a sensitivity to nature and an awareness of its presence is both a ritual and a desire among the villagers.

The road from the Engelskrone winds down through hills and terraces to the upper section of the village. Rebhausen is shaped roughly in the form of an L, the vertical section rising up the flank of the Engelskrone for approximately one kilometer, the longitudinal section trailing along the bottom edge about the same distance and spilling out into the plain. Where the road enters Rebhausen it becomes Baumstrasse, the main street of Oberdorf, the upper section of Rebhausen which was once a separate village. The homes press closely on Baumstrasse, each side an

3

almost uninterrupted line of colorless, grey-brown stucco constructions with steeply pitched tile roofs and small, curtained windows. Most of the side streets which lead off from Braumstrasse are not paved. There is no business district in Oberdorf. The stores and shops are there—groceries, construction company, bakery, butcher shop, dry goods store, restaurant—but their signs are unobtrusive and the shops blend into the line of symetrical, monotonous, two-story residential construction.

Baumstrasse intersects Herrenstrasse at the bottom of the slope. To the left and north along Herrenstrasse is the main part of town—the *Rathaus,* [town hall], the school, the churches, the wine cooperative, shops, and homes; to the right, more

A main street in Rebhausen.

homes, a restaurant, and then open fields. Straight ahead are more homes and the industrial development. The latter is within the village limits, but to the long-time residents it is *draussen* [out there], a presence natives view with mixed feelings.

FARMING

One of the first comments I heard a native make about an inhabitant of the factory housing development was, "Der lebt von der Hand in den Mund—hat kein Grundstück." [He lives from hand to mouth—doesn't own any land.] It is an indictment rooted deep in the historical and cultural consciousness of the village. Land—its ownership, distribution, and use—is a fundamental concern of Rebhausen natives. The dynamics of this concern are structured not only by the *Wein-*

bau [the cultivation of grapes] ecology but also by a sense of the past which most natives share. They know the conditions of village life have been shaped by developments with distant antecedents.

Rebhausen is an old village, the first mention of it having been discovered in records of land transactions made in A.D. 769. Its early history is sketchy. The area surrounding the village is considered to be a rather rich source of prehistoric artifacts. When it was partially covered by glaciers and plant life along the Rhine was sparse, herds of deer and wild horses had to roam for food. The hills of the Engelskrone offered a good lookout for hunters. The oldest finds, fragments of pots and arrowheads, date back to the Neolithic period. There is more evidence of the subsequent Roman settlement (A.D. 0–260). Gold coins and remnants of Roman roads and pottery have been discovered in the area. Most important, the cultivation of grapes was initiated during the Roman occupation. In the third century, the Alemannen began to migrate from Brandenburg to the region and by the end of the fifth century exercised complete control.

The Middle Ages was unsettling. Ownership of land and political control of the region were unstable. Political developments in the early Middle Ages were shaped by Baden nobility who owned considerable territory. Land in the village changed hands frequently. By the fifteenth century portions of Rebhausen and Oberdorf, an adjoining village, belonged to the Baden nobility, portions to Austrian nobility. This division had particular significance in the latter part of the sixteenth century when the Baden nobility embraced the Evangelical confession, thereby committing two-third of both villages to Protestantism. The remaining third was retained by the Austrians and continued Catholic.

The condition of divided ownership created problems of administration and taxation, but until the Austrian portion reverted to Baden ownership (with the Peace of Pressburg of 1805) little was done to resolve such problems. In the early part of the nineteenth century steps were taken to affect a merger; economic problms made it necessary but religious and geographic divisions made it difficult. The merger of the two villages was finally completed in 1838, with due attention to establishing a harmonious relationship between the two confessions.

Although the absence of industry in the nineteenth century and first half of the twentieth century is a primary explanation for the lack of population growth, natives are more conscious of the debilitating effects of war and a series of disastrous crop failures. Village records report that in 1817, 113 people started to emigrate to the United States but got only as far as Holland. Many of them returned to Rebhausen as beggars, having lost all of their belongings. In the 1850s the village helped finance a group of 225 to emigrate to Algeria, because the land in Rehbhausen could not support them. Although the village enjoyed periods of prosperity during the twentieth century, the two wars and the economic collapse which followed in each instance were traumatic experiences not easily forgotten. In Rebhausen today, war and poverty are the predominant themes which natives invoke to summarize the past.

Although the land has often failed them, it remains both the symbol and reality of cultural persistence, an enduring value that can survive wars and inflation and that has meaning which transcends the logic of efficient agricultural practices. Land ownership is extremely fragmented; no farm is one continuous holding. Of the total village area of 1299 hectares (1 hectare = 2.47 acres), 955 hectares are used for farming operations. Within this farm area there are 8494 separate pieces of property, the average size being for meadows 12 ar (1 ar = 1076 square feet), for cultivated land 10 ar, and for *Weinbau* under 4 ar. The 955 hectares are distributed among 436 separate farm operations, 183 full-time and 253 part-time.

Of the 955 hectares, approximately 430 are devoted to raising wheat, barley, oats, potatoes, and turnips. There are 340 hectares maintained as meadowland primarily for hay crops. Grape holdings total approximately 124 hectares. A variety of fruit trees are scattered throughout the village and located in small plots. Apples, pears, cherries, peaches, plums, and other fruits are grown. Garden crops include cabbage, lettuce, carrots, tomatoes, and celery.

Pigs are the primary source of meat. Families with even the minimal barn or shed facilities raise at least one or two pigs for slaughter and personal consumption. What remains of the fast disappearing cattle are either milk cows or, in several instances, oxen. Goats provide milk for several families. Chickens and/or rabbits are common to almost all farm operations, the former rather noted as an ever-present source of irritation among neighbors. The average Rebhausen native exploits every source of food supply that his time will allow.

Several of the full-time farm operations have as many as twenty-five different plots. The pattern of land ownership reflects the impact of the ancient tradition of *Erbteilung* [the equal division of land among all children, sons and daughters]. The tradition was binding on both generations. The older generation provided for a legal, equitable distribution; the younger generation was bound by tradition and sanction to accept the distribution. For a young man, however committed to an urban life and disinterested in farming, to sell his inheritance was a deep affront to the core value of the culture. This tradition functioned to support and nurture productive relationships within the extended family[1] and to bind the family to the land.

The centrality of the tradition to the value system and life of the village is reflected in its dysfunctional aspects. The practice not only rendered farming operations increasingly more inefficient but also created personal hardships. The sons worked the land with the fathers; it was their livelihood and they learned no other vocation. But with the distribution of property the farm had to support a number of individual family units rather than just a single, extended family. Consequently sons were often forced to find part-time work to supplement the farm income. In one ironic sense the tradition created conditions which made industry for the village necessary and inevitable.

Erbteilung continued into the 1930s. In 1933 the Nazi regime promulgated the *Erbhofgesetz* making it illegal in this region to divide farms greater than six or seven hectares in size. The division of smaller farms was no issue since they were not considered economically viable. The process of division had prevailed for so many decades that only one Rebhausen farm fell under the law (as a result the

---

[1] In Rebhausen three generations in one house is typical among farm families. During peak farm operations, especially the harvest, uncles, aunts, and cousins move in and out of larger work groups as the need arises.

farmer acquired the name, *Erbhofbauer*). A policy of discouraging fragmentation and encouraging consolidation is today an integral part of agricultural legislation. State law assures priority to farmers in the purchase of farm land and requires that the distribution of land through inheritance not reduce the size of the basic farm unit below 4.5 hectares. At the same time a program of subsidy and low interest loans is directed toward encouraging farmers to move out of the village onto the land. Two cases of this type of development are underway in Rebhausen. The homes are modern and well equipped. The barns are laid out and use of the fields planned to make possible an efficient, mechanized farm operation. But these steps were taken before the process of consolidation had been completed. Consequently these farmers must cover even more distance in traveling to and from their farm

Harvesting grapes.

property. For this observable reason, and because the whole concept is foreign to the basic and traditional pattern of village life, Rebhausen farmers tend to be skeptical about such change. Nevertheless, over a period of several decades the trend toward consolidation is perceptible.

Weinbau. A 4.5 hectare farm is large enough to make a decent living if at least half of it is devoted to *Weinbau, Weinbau* in Rebhausen is the central ecological theme of the village culture, although of the total land area used in farming operations only about one-seventh is for *Weinbau*. It is the basic economic activity and the only one profitable enough to sustain the pattern of land ownership. As the central theme of village life and the ranking economic activity it has broad, intricately related social and cultural ramifications. The practice of *Weinbau* establishes, as nothing else can, the validity of individuals and families as meaningful participants in the village life. It creates and sustains a rhythm of social interaction which constantly renews a sense of village unity. Meetings to discuss problems of *Weinbau* or to consider the progress and policies of the local wine co-operative involve potentially most Rebhausen natives. It affects the life of the school, especially the allocation of vacation periods. One of the longest vacation periods is the month of October, the time of harvest when children are needed in the fields. *Weinbau* is a recurring theme in the songs the *Gesangverein* [men's chorus] sings and in the jokes, anecdotes and aphorisms which are a part of the currency of informal social exchange. A visit in the home does not really get underway until a pitcher of the host's own wine is obtained from the cellar and a toast offered to the health of all. No meeting in the *Turnhalle* [school gymnasium] proceeds without wine, and the physical arrangements facilitate its proper use and enjoyment. Instead of chairs, rows of tables are set up and one of the local restaurant owners is contracted to serve wine, bread and, on many occasions, hot sausage.

Since *Weinbau* and the wine market are the key to the level of village prosperity, they are the object of constant speculation and concern. Before I came to know Rebhausen, I had been told that the village had been traditionally isolated from modern economic developments and was only beginning to awaken from the slow pace of rural life. I was therefore unprepared for the sensitivity natives displayed toward national and supra-national developments in economic exchange. The prospect of greatly increased competition from French wine in an unprotected market is an impending development of great concern.

The typical reaction to the changes which the evolution of the European Common Market may produce is neither isolationist nor protectionist. The basic position of the Rebhausen native seems to be affected primarily by the war experience. Any supra-national organization that can create better, more harmonious relations among the nations of Europe and more particularly between Germany and France is welcomed. A free market is recognized as integral to the success of such a hope. Consequently, with respect to their own competitive position, the prevailing attitude is one of urgency. Rebhausen has to prepare for the impending change. Thus, before industrialization became a fact, the village was awakening to the demands and complications of change.

Prior to World War II the traditional *Weinbau* methods had changed little except in marketing procedures. Before 1934 the farmers harvested and processed the grapes, made their own wine, and sold it primarily to restaurant owners. They were vulnerable to market fluctuations and to the whims of individual purchasers. In 1934 the Rebhausen wine co-operative was established, providing a centralized system of processing and sale. Membership meant that the farmer harvested the grapes and delivered them to the co-operative.

This innovation was a blessing for the farmer, but membership was slow in developing. Joining involves a certain sacrifice of independence and the elimination of the most meaningful part of the entire *Weinbau* process—pressing the grapes and nurturing the juice in casks through the fermentation point until a full-bodied wine is established. But membership has increased steadily since the war. In 1965 it had reached approximately 300, representing 85 percent of *Weinbau* farmers. An increasing number are turning to the co-operative because the attraction of shift work in the factory leaves them less time for farming. In practically all cases those who join the co-operative continue to make enough wine for home consumption through the year.

The establishment of the co-operative has alleviated complicated processing and marketing procedures, but it has not changed two basic conditions which seriously restrict the efficiency of *Weinbau*—the pattern of land ownership and the increasing inaccessibility of the plots themselves. The fragmentation of ownership means that an inordinate amount of time is spent assembling, dismantling and moving equipment from one plot to another. The problem is most serious when the vines have to be sprayed. Whether a portable spraying unit packed on the back is used or

New grape plantings—after terraces have been leveled and holdings consolidated.

a system of hoses attached to a large tank (the size and location of the plot determines the procedure), the time factor weighs heavily on the efficiency of *Weinbau*.

Inaccessibility, in terms of the topography of the plots and the roads and paths leading to them, is another problem. The region itself is hilly, and because the plots are small the network of terraces is intricate. Growing areas are scattered. This condition increases the time required to tend and harvest the grapes. The avenues of access are also in many cases unsatisfactory. The major roads are narrow and deeply eroded. Efficient use cannot always be made of tractors. Some terraces are so inaccessible that they can only be reached through precipitous foot paths. Harvesting is tedious and time consuming. The grapes are cut, dumped into a long, cylindrical container, packed on the back, and carried down the path to a wagon.

Flurbereinigung. For several decades a program of *Flurbereinigung* [land consolidation and access improvement] has been developing in the region. When applied to the cultivation of grapes, the program consists of pulling up the vines, stakes, and fences, bulldozing the small, irregular system of terraces in order to create large, continuous terraces, consolidating and reassigning plots to make ownership contiguous in any one area, and building asphalt roads to and through the area. The process requires four to six months, and the state reimburses farmers up to 65 percent of the cost of new plants. But the labor required to prepare the land for bulldozing—that is, pulling up the stakes and clearing the land of personal property—must be provided by the owner. New plants require three years of growth before they begin to bear fruit. So the crucial factor for the farmer is the loss of three years of income from the grape harvest.

The process when instituted seldom means the total loss of income from *Weinbau* since it involves at any one time only a limited area of grape plots. If a typical farm is approximately five hectares in size with two hectares devoted to *Weinbau,* the probability is that no more than one-third of a hectare will be tied up in the process. The net profit on one-third of a hectare is estimated at 4000 DM (1 DM = $0.25) or 12,000 DM over a three-year period. State subsidies in connection with *Flurbereinigung* reduce the loss to about 2500 DM per year.

During 1964–1965 the village was deeply involved in the question of *Flurbereinigung.* The events which took place in connection with the issue and the previous experiences of Rebhausen natives with *Flurbereinigung* are relevant not only to an understanding of *Weinbau* but also to an assessment of the forces in village life which affect the prospect and process of change.

Although the *Flurbereinigung* movement predates World War II, the origins of developments in Rebhausen lie in the war itself. The prospect of war with France made the hilly region of the Engelskrone overlooking the Rhine River and French territory beyond of prime military importance. Rebhausen was not affected directly by preparations, and it did not experience appreciable damage to buildings or land during the war. Villages with more strategic locations suffered considerable damage to terraces as a result of gun emplacements and bombardments. For these villages *Flurbereinigung* was logical and persuasive.

Warnings about the effect of the European Common Market on the sale of wine and the more immediate visibility of *Flurbereinigung* progress in nearby villages combined to foster a sense of urgency in Rebhausen. Natives were convinced the village was at least ten years behind in the improvement of *Weinbau.* Lack of progress is to be explained in part by the kind of experience the village had had with *Flurbereinigung* during the past decade. The first effort, in 1952, involving 11 hectares, was almost a complete failure. The specie of grape recommended for planting in the area consolidated was found unsuitable to the soil. The vine produced a rich foliage but no fruit. After two years the plants had to be replaced with a different specie. Consequently, it was five years before farmers owning land in this area could begin to recapture their loss.

The second attempt, in 1954, was more successful. Only 3.5 hectares were involved, the specie was suited to the soil, and the grape harvest at the end of the third year justified the investment. Nevertheless, this experience also left a residue of irritation and discontentment. The area consolidated contained sections which had already been privately improved by farmers who had taken the initiative and made their own financial sacrifice.

The third attempt, involving between 25 and 30 hectares, was successful technically speaking but, like the other two, unsettling—in this case because the opposition was more organized. To acquire sufficient approval to institute *Flurbereinigung,* officials have two methods from which to choose, *Klassisch* [traditional]² or *Freiwillig* [voluntary]. The former requires approval of 75 percent of all the owners, at which point the state takes an active part in supervising the process. Since, in this case, 25 percent of the owners can be coerced into participating, the procedure is much longer and more expensive. State and county officials are necessarily more deeply involved, a fact which adds to the expense. In addition, because the potential or real opposition can be as high as 25 percent, opportunities are provided for hearings and appeals from decisions made. With voluntary *Flurbereinigung,* 98 percent of the owners must approve. When the necessary signatures are obtained, the process can be instituted and carried through with relatively little intervention on the part of higher authorities. The village usually hires a private concern to implement the decision. In Rebhausen the first three experiences with *Flurbereinigung* had been "forced," and the last of the three, in 1956–57, had provoked heated opposition from among the 25 percent not signing. A lawyer had been hired to defend their interests.

Between 1957 and 1964 there had been little official activity with respect to instituting another *Flurbereinigung.* The leadership in this area, as in most aspects of village life, fell to the mayor. Through the 1950s he organized meetings to encourage the *Flurbereinigung* movement, but he was also absorbed in negotiations to bring a factory to the village. Some of the natives claimed Rebhausen was ten years behind other Engelskrone villages because of the mayor's preoccupation with industrialization to the neglect of the farmer and farming interests. Whatever the circumstances the mayor, the factory firmly established, began in late 1964 to agitate for the consolidation of a 32-hectare area adjacent to a site (belonging to the adjacent village) where *Flurbereinigung* was almost completed and where for some months the operation had been to Rebhausen natives both audible and visible.

Early in October the mayor convened a town meeting to consider *Flurbereinigung.* The *Turnhalle* [school gymnasium] was full—over 300 farmers were there, a few with their wives who collected at a corner table near the front. It was a kind of observation station where they could be at the meeting but not in it. The mayor was primed; he had collected a staff of specialists, politicians, and administrative officials to help him argue the case for *Flurbereinigung.* He started the meeting by reminding the citizens that the last town meeting that had attracted such a crowd was the one called to consider approval of a site for the factory. He told them they all had a chance to vote for progress, that Rebhausen was not hopelessly behind in the improvement of *Weinbau,* but that action had to be taken soon to match the progress other villages were making in preparation for the European Common Market.

---

² Juxtaposed with the voluntary approach this method has for natives a meaning of "forced."

His first speaker was a respresentative to the state legislature. Representative Weber discussed the relationship of the legislature to the subsidies available to a village choosing to initiate *Flurbereinigung*. He reminded them the money was there; it had been appropriated. But he warned them that they could not count on it indefinitely. As long as China was diverting the U.S.A. and the U.S.S.R. from their own animosities, Germany could enjoy reasonable political and international stability, but a change in international affairs could create budgetary strains and force a cutback in subsidy appropriations. The conclusion was clear, Weber said; use the money while you can.

A specialist from the regional office of the state department of agriculture described successful experiences with *Flurbereinigung* in other villages. He pointed out that, like it or not, the younger generation of farmers, most of whom would be part-time, would not be content with outmoded farming practices. *Weinbau* had to change and improve or become atrophied. An engineer from a *Flurbereinigung* institute presented charts and statistics relative to improvement of the area under consideration. Finally a state official urged the farmers to approve *Flurbereinigung* and initiate the process as soon as possible.

At the end of the speeches the mayor declared a 10-minute recess which lasted over 30 minutes as the farmers crowded around the maps and charts and talked with officials. As soon as the mayor called the meeting to order, he proposed that two committees be elected—one to collect the necessary signatures and the other to hear complaints. There was an immediate objection from the floor. A farmer claimed the mayor was proceeding too fast and ignoring the democratic process. People, he said, had come to the meeting to consider, first of all, whether or not to approve *Flurbereinigung*. Therefore, a vote should be taken on the basic issue. The objection elicited considerable clapping and shouts of approval. The mayor reminded them that at a previous meeting in April the issue of *Flurbereinigung* had been considered and approval registered. In response several farmers took the floor to point out that they had not attended the meeting; others claimed the April meeting was only exploratory and that basic approval had not been obtained.

The mayor pushed on and asked for other comments and questions. A factory worker rose to urge that *Flurbereinigung* be approved, and the mayor praised him for supporting the best interests of the farmers. At this point the meeting was beginning to unravel. The noise level was increasing; groups were engaged in heated conversations. Several people were on their feet talking at the same time. The mayor frequently had to gavel for order, and the ladies up front were trying to help him by shushing the men.

The issue was finally resolved by a vote or rather a maneuver. The mayor asked all those opposed to *Flurbereinigung* to stand up and be counted. About thirty men stood up. He declared the issue approved and asked for committee nominations. As a man's name was called out, the mayor asked if there was any opposition to the nomination. If no disapproval was expressed, the mayor declared the man elected. When the committees were formed, they were instructed to begin collecting signatures and the meeting was closed. It was a significant development in the village's confrontation of change, but it was complicated and to some degree obscured by the characteristics of the meeting itself.

The mayor hoped that the necessary signatures could be obtained within a few months and the *Flurbereinigung* process initiated and completed in time to set out new plantings in the spring. Sixty percent of the signatures were obtained almost immediately, but for almost one-third of the owners there were reasons to wait or to be unalterably opposed to the process. The young, full-time farmers generally support *Flurbereinigung* enthusiastically; they understand and accept its relevance to their future. Older farmers who through the years have acquired leadership responsibilities in the community also support the process.

Opposition or skepticism has a variety of explanations. There are farmers who still nurture bitterness and disappointment as a result of earlier experiences. A large percentage of those who did not sign immediately are small owners, many of whom were working in the factory. Consolidation is considered no particular advantage for a person whose holding is 40 ar or less. He knows his land will be reduced by at least 10 percent to provide for an improved system of roads. With full-time work in the factory he is not pressed to modernize his farming operation. There are marginal farmers, often elderly people whose sons have left the land to work in the factory, who cannot afford the three-year loss of income, needed to improve the plots they own in the area. Finally, all land owners are anxious that consolidation not leave them with land of an inferior quality or location compared to what they previously held.

These were the hopes, fears, and uncertainties that faced the mayor and his committee as they set out to persuade the additional 38 percent to sign. The conditions and forces operating in the process of approving and carrying through *Flurbereinigung* disturbed the normally quiet, routine village life. Implicit cultural directives became overtly operational as the process continued. *Flurbereinigung* seemed imperative to a majority of landowners, and the voluntary method the most appealing instrument of implementation. It was intrinsically democratic, comparatively free of administrative intervention by higher authorities, and potentially reflective of the corporate will of the village. At the same time the almost total unanimity required to initiate *Flurbereinigung* created strains and provoked a negative or at least doubtful expression of village unity.

Those who opposed *Flurbereinigung* were subjected to considerable pressure. There was no intimidation, no threat of recrimination. But the pressure was persistent; the mayor invoked all the prestige and influence of his office to persuade them to sign. The committee began by calling on individuals. They went singly or in small groups to visit the farmers in their homes. They accosted individuals at public meetings and urged them to sign. If that was not successful, the mayor called groups into his office to talk to them and finally resorted to individual conferences. His appeal, he said, was direct: "You can't stand in the way of progress. You absolutely have to cooperate and come along with the rest of us. It's the only fair thing to do." These negotiations continued into 1965, past the time when plantings could be made. The delay provoked a frustration with the democratic process. Some of the farmers felt the village leadership was too humane—that too much respect was afforded those who did not want to sign. They claimed other villages were making more progress because they refused to tolerate such delays.

By early summer the necessary signatures were obtained and plans were made to begin *Flurbereinigung* in the fall. In a positive sense, the experience redressed the grievances and discontent which farmers had experienced with the process in the past decade. More important, it gave the village valuable practice in making decisions vital to a productive adjustment to change. In a negative sense, the experience created ambivalent feelings about the efficacy of the democratic procedure and encouraged the conviction that the decision-making process, especially where the issue was basic to the prosperity of the village, should somehow be more coercive and less tolerant of deviant behavior.

REBHAUSEN AND INDUSTRY

In 1815 Rebhausen had a population of 2000; in 1958, the year the factory was established, 2388. Six years later, as I began the study, the population had risen to approximately 3000, and, when I departed after eleven months, Rebhausen had acquired almost 400 more residents. The mayor predicted that in the next decade, with the fulfillment of the development plan, the population would be close to 7000. The change is particularly significant because the size of the village has remained constant for over a century, as the following figures indicate.

Year	*Population*
1815	2000
1875	2154
1925	2119
1939	2197
1946	2191
1948	2305
1955	2303
1957	2354
1959	2504
1961	2732
1964	3372

An examination of movement in and out of the village following World War II points to a change in both the tempo and content of the population growth. In the period between 1945 and 1958 the population remained relatively constant, increasing by only 150 since 1875. The village was unaffected during this period by the tremendous refugee movement from eastern and northern Germany to the western and southern sections of the country. Rebhausen had neither housing nor work to offer refugees. But the factory changed these conditions. For example, in March 1955, there was a net population increase of 1; 9 Germans moved in and 8 moved out. The majority of these individuals were classified as either unskilled labor or housewives. Ten years later, in March of 1965, there was a net population increase during the month of 53. Those moving in included 35 Germans, 18 Italians, 1 Austrian, 1 Brazilian, 2 Turks and 5 Yugoslavians. Eight Germans and 1 Italian moved out. The predominant vocational categories of those moving in were skilled labor and administrative personnel. Of those moving out the majority were un-skilled labor. The factory was not only affecting changes in economic activities but also creating in the life of the village new and alien communities.

The factory, a chemical concern manufacturing a wide assortment of products, now employs over 900 workers at least half of whom are residents of Rebhausen. Of this number, approximately two-fifths are natives; the rest, newcomers. Up-wards of 400 workers and executive personnel commute each day to the factory from over 40 communities in the surrounding area. The company sends out daily a fleet of buses to pick up workers. There are, in addition, an increasing number of foreign workers—in 1965, 103. They include 42 Brazilians, 48 Turks, 8 Italians, 1 Pole, 1 Yugoslavian, 1 Indian, 1 Australian and 1 Frenchman. With the factory working three shifts at full capacity, it is expected that within a few years the work force will increase to about 1200.

Because their folk culture had never provided a model, the factory constitutes a commanding social and economic presence for Rebhausen natives. The village has known industry on a very small scale, but these operations were, in most instances, unable to survive economic fluctuations. A cigar factory was established in the early 1900s but had to close after several decades of operation. A toy concern lasted only six years. A stone quarry operation, with the quarry located up in the northwest-ern part of the village and the crushing-sorting plant in the southeastern corner, employed as many as 60 men but now employs 17, primarily because of mechaniza-tion. These small concerns did not disrupt the portrait of Rebhausen as a rural, farm community culturally isolated from the population center to the southeast.

The region of which Rebhausen is a part has long been identified as economical-ly backward and culturally distinctive, nurturing a simple, individualistic, and un-sophisticated way of life. Consequently, although before 1958 as many as 400 na-tives commuted to jobs in nearby communities, village life itself had not encom-passed any industrial institution such as the factory.

The chemical factory was established in 1958, the culmination of six years of effort to acquire industry. Primary credit for attracting the factory to Rebhausen be-longs to the mayor. The role he played in the process is suggestive not only of the power and influence a mayor possesses in a southwest German village, but also of the leadership a public official, sensitive to the direction of change, can exercise within the milieu of a culture weighted with restraining pressures of tradition. The mayor has both executive and judicial powers and responsibilities. He is an elected official, for eight years the first term, for twelve years in succeeding terms. The long tenure tends to perpetuate him in office. In the Rebhausen area most of the mayors had already served one term and many of them had run unopposed in the last election. The almost infinite number of announcements, instructions, remind-ers, and warnings which flow from his office (he acts as an administrative agent for the county and state governments) maintain and reinforce his centrality in the struc-ture of village government. He is empowered to intervene in matters of immediate importance to the average citizen. A newcomer's first obligation is to go to the *Ra-thaus* and register; he cannot remain in the village unless he does. Questions of housing, still a pressing, sensitive concern of the inhabitants, are within his administrative domain. For individuals involved in neighborhood disputes or other forms of civil strife, the reconciliation process must begin in his office. There are, in short, few aspects of village life in which he does not involve himself and the prestige of his office.

The *Gemeinderat* [village council], the legislative organ composed of twelve persons elected for four-year terms on a rotating basis, must vote on a great many questions which the mayor is charged with administering. They can, therefore, affectively influence and contain the use the mayor makes of his powers. But the *Gemeinderat* meets once every two weeks; the mayor is at work every day. Mayor Watzinger carried out his responsibilities with bombastic energy. The *Gemeinderat,* composed primarily of elderly farmers, was no match for him.

The mayor was first elected to office in 1948 and re-elected in 1956. He is a native, a farmer's son who had left the farm to his two brothers before the war and started commercial training and work in a nearby city. He spent several years as a clerk and bookkeeper in a cigar concern. After the war (he served five years in the *Wehrmacht,* [the army], most of which was spent on the Russian front), he decided to apply for the position of town clerk and treasurer. He was appointed to the position in 1946, and after two years of service his record was such to qualify him, so many people in the village felt, for the office of mayor. The election in 1948 gave him an overwhelming victory.

From the beginning of his first term of office he was obsessed, he said, with bringing industry to Rebhausen; he was sure the village could not grow and prosper without it. He wanted jobs in Rebhausen for the 400 natives who left the village each day to work in nearby communities and for the sons of farmers who, with mechanization, were interested in and able to seek additional opportunities for employment. He wanted industry in order to boost local businesses and trades. He wanted to increase the village income, to expand the tax base and create revenue for village improvements.

At the southwestern corner of the village were 2.5 hectares of land, owned by the village and rented to farmers. The land was flat, of only average value for farming, and adjacent to the small railroad line which links Rebhausen with Waldstadt. It was an ideal site for a factory. In 1952 he began to seek contacts with potential users, offering use of the land without rent. When his first lead developed, he called a town meeting and, to increase the likelihood of good attendance, arranged an auction of firewood just before the meeting. His purpose was to inform the citizenry of developments, to solicit their approval for the project, and to have a committee appointed to help him proceed with contacts. (Important community issues are, according to state law, to be decided by a town meeting; either a two-thirds vote of the *Gemeinderat* or a petition with the signatures of 25 percent of eligible voters is needed to place an issue before the town meeting.)

Support for his interest in industry was not unanimous, especially among the farmers. From their standpoint the site was good farm land. Rebhausen had always been a farming community and should remain one; the site could be used not only for farming but also for home construction; the village did not need industry and whatever industry it acquired would probably be destroyed in a war. But the *Gemeinderat,* most of whom were farmers, supported him. They had visited industrialized areas in the region and had seen what industry could mean to a community. The mayor remembered the trip vividly: *"Das habe ich mir angesehen und gedacht, aus Rebhausen kann man da auch etwas machen,"* [I saw all that and thought, Rebhausen can do it too].

His first prospects ended in failure—so disastrous that the whole project was almost buried by the reaction. The village committed 20,000 DM toward the purchase of machines to aid a Swiss businessman in setting up a shoe factory. But the owner was intent on acquiring title to the land and then reselling it. He absconded with the money (fortunately covered by insurance), and the mayor had to face the citizenry and those who had insisted the project was wrong for the community. The second prospect was a paper factory. The problems of water supply, drainage, and waste disposal involved such protracted discussions with officials from the county and neighboring villages that negotiations collapsed. The third prospect, a fountain pen concern, went bankrupt in the midst of negotiations. Each time the mayor reported the results to the village. Each time he exhorted them to be patient: *"Eines Tages wird es dann schon klappen,"* [One day we'll succeed].

The longer decisive action was delayed, the more frustrated and impatient many natives became. They had, to be sure, participated in the original decision. Sanction had been registered at the town meeting through a majority decision valid because at least one-half of all eligible voters were in attendance. The mayor had surmounted that obstacle but pre-empting the land for community use was a more painful process. For the present lessees, he had to find other land, most of which was more distant from the village and often of an inferior quality. As soon as the village had reclaimed the land, he had oats planted on the site. So the village waited and watched the land produce oats, and the farmers pictured a factory there, occupying the land and attracting the few workers still available as farm labor.

In 1958 contact was established with the home office of a chemical concern. By now the mayor was advertising in big city newspapers and, with the help of county officials, he had created an interest in the Rebhausen site. After complicated financial negotiations, involving state officials, agreement was reached and a contract signed. The firm was committed to build or return the land to the village. The building program had to include a housing development, some units of which were to be made available to the community for general housing needs. The community was committed to fill in portions of the site that were marshy, to survey and show the presence of an adequate labor supply, and to begin a program of community improvement designed not only to meet the basic needs of a growing population but also to make the village more attractive to people moving from urban, industrial centers. The factory began creating jobs and a way of life that the village had not experienced.

THE EFFECT OF THE FACTORY

The changes that the factory affected in the appearance of the village and the conveniences the village now offers are evident to a native. A comparison of the

1958 and 1963 budgets provides further proof of change. In 1963 the income from the sewer system tax was 8425 DM and from garbage collection 7646 DM. The 1958 budget contained no such items. There was no sewer system; outside privies were typical. Garbage collection had been no problem. Most people farmed, part- or full-time, and maintained farm animals. Garbage was easily disposed of within farm operations. Empty cans were no problem; canned goods were seldom found in the stores. Three years after the establishment of the factory, the community had to institute a system of garbage collection, and by 1965 garbage disposal was a problem that the community itself could not satisfactorily solve. Disposal was arranged with a private company.

The increased population and rising standard of living is reflected in other budgetary items. Home property tax collections went from 10,000 DM to 29,000 DM; farm property tax collections from 28,000 DM to 45,000 DM; business taxes from 10,000 DM to 44,000 DM. Expenditures also reflected change. The cost of village administration climbed from 26,387 DM to 74,765 DM. Before 1958 the mayor had run the office himself and was his own secretary. By 1963 he had three secretaries and an administrative assistant. In 1958 the village spent 10,575 DM on street repairs and improvements; in 1963, 128,257 DM. In 1958 only the two main streets were paved; by 1963 the program of improvement was reaching into the small side streets which wind through the residential areas.

A comparison of total village expenditures over a 50-year period is indicative of the dramatic change the village has experienced in the past five years:

Year	Expenditures
1915	120,120.58 DM
1926	114,171.44
1930	74,489.05
1941	254,396.87
1960	465,883.00
1964	936,000.00

The budget for 1965 was, the mayor felt, a significant development; it was over 1,000,000 DM.

New housing in Rebhausen is located primarily at the site adjacent to the factory. By the summer of 1964 over 56 apartment units had been built of two- and three-story construction, long and rectangular, with windows and balconies breaking the expanse of gray stucco. These units were financed by the factory and most of them reserved for factory personnel. A building co-operative financed several more apartment houses, and there are on the site approximately 20 two and one-half story, three-unit homes built by private individuals: natives who wanted to invest their savings in rental property or who were ready to abandon their old, cramped housing. In most cases the owner occupies the first floor and rents the upper two stories.

In five years of operation the factory has made a noticeable impact on patterns of work and vocational interests. By 1965 there were over 200 natives working in the factory, most of whom sought employment shortly after the factory opened. The mayor had hoped to create jobs in Rebhausen for natives who normally worked in adjoining villages and cities. The following statistics indicate the changes taking place.

Year	Workers Commuting to Rebhausen	Workers Commuting from Rebhausen
1950	9	232
1957	10	408
1961	285	355
1964	352	260

Mechanization is an important factor in making factory work attractive to Rebhausen natives. At the end of World War II, there were only four tractors in the village. By 1964 almost all full-time farmers and at least 50 percent of the part-

The housing development.

time farmers owned tractors. *Weinbau* procedures are steadily being improved. Motorized spray units make it possible to complete in 30 minutes a job that had ordinarily taken four hours. The vines are now much more accessible. The plants had traditionally been tied to single posts and the rows planted close together. In recent years a network of posts and wires has been instituted, and the rows placed farther apart. Production has increased and cultivation made much simpler.

Mechanization has rendered cattle obsolete. They are rapidly disappearing from the village and with them the time-consuming chore of gathering fodder each day. Horses are of use during rainy weather on steep terraces, but they, too, are disappearing and are maintained more for sentimental or recreational purposes.

The cause and effect relationship between work at the factory and mechanization is not unidirectional. The small, part-time farmer earns money in the factory and uses part of it to mechanize his operation. But only with mechanization can he work in the factory and maintain a farm at the same time. Shift work is admirably suited to the economic needs of the small farmer. Shift assignments are rotated every two weeks; a part-time farmer can always find time during the day, whatever the shift, for farm work.

The adjustment to the demands of factory work have not been easy for the natives. Two basic values in the native culture are alien to factory work—a love of nature and a sense of independence, both fulfilled in the life of a farmer. Factory executives reported that absenteeism was, in the first few years, a problem. If farm work were pressing and the weather suitable, a part-time farmer might decide not to report to work. A consciousness of idle machines and lost man-hours was not a part of his cultural domain.

Social changes.   The presence and growing size of the housing development has not created productive channels of interaction. Reference to the development as *Draussen* is both a convenient locational designation and a socially separational term. Some natives, most of whom are working in the factory, have moved into the development. A number of teachers prefer the location with its modern construction, and there are families who have moved out from Waldstadt. Most of the residents, however, are employees of the factory and strangers to Rebhausen, refugees and migrants from every part of Germany and former German territories.

These strangers came to work in the factory. They came because the factory offered employment commensurate with their vocational training and aspirations and provided housing acceptable to their family needs. They accepted employment because the move represented an actual or potential advancement—particularly at the executive or foreman level—with a growing company whose parent operation in west central Germany was well established in an expanding field. They left behind them the conveniences and sophistication of urban life and, in this respect, were consoled only by the nearby presence of Waldstadt. In some cases they had decided to accept employment in Rebhausen because of the rural setting, the immediacy of the natural environment which their children could enjoy; but, in no instance, have newcomers expressed, as a basic motive, the desire to live and participate in the life of the village.

Village life is not completely alien to them. Traditional days and seasons of celebration—Christmas, Good Friday, Easter, the First of May, confirmation of eighth graders—are shared alike by natives and newcomers. There are, however, deeply meaningful moments of celebration, peculiar to the native or regional culture, which newcomers find amusing and view with detachment. The wedding procession, on foot, through the village to the church and back to the home of the bride's parents is one such tradition. Indeed, the early morning wedding day revelry—firecrackers and loud explosions outside the groom's window—has provoked complaints from the housing development. The mayor found it necessary to restrict the initiation of such revelry to a reasonable hour.

Neither the celebrations which unite the two groups nor those which separate them are predictive of the kind of relationship which is developing. The younger generation of natives are displaying less interest in maintaining the traditional village culture. More of them are marrying outside the village, a practice that a decade previously had been considered acceptable but undesirable and that before the war was a real affront to the village. Fewer of them are submitting to the wedding procession; they have cars. Traditions, especially native celebrations, which to the newcomers seem provincial are becoming unacceptable to younger natives, a development accelerated by the presence of this new social group but not the direct result of it.

A large majority of natives who sought employment at the factory entered as unskilled or semi-skilled workers or as clerks and bookkeepers in the administrative department. A much smaller number, with established trades such as electrician or tool-and-die worker, also chose employment in the factory. Several natives occupy responsible administrative positions in the purchasing and accounting departments. Almost all the executive personnel and foremen are newcomers. Consequently, vocational patterns among natives and newcomers, as well as basic differences in life styles, affect the quality and quantity of social interaction between the two groups.

The vocational content of the social structure of the two groups is indicative of factors discouraging interaction. The job hierarchy in the factory is carefully ranked by function and responsibility. Two broad categories, *Arbeiter* [blue-collar worker] and *Angestellte* [white-collar worker] serve to separate administrative and executive personnel from the main body of workers. The range in the latter group extends from a filing clerk to plant manager; within it there is a distribution of prestige based on function and responsibility and typical of an industrial operation. This differentiation is reinforced by factors outside the operation of the factory: type of housing, place of residence, social activities. Consequently, among newcomers themselves there is little social interaction across vocational levels.

The life style of factory executives who have chosen to live in Rebhausen is very visible to natives.[3] Prosperous homes have been built on a secluded hillside, a newly designated residential section of the village. Several of the new homes are ranch-style construction—modern and foreign to traditional native construction. Furthermore, the process of zoning this particular section for residential purposes and of granting permits to build provoked the feeling among some natives that special attention was being given the newcomers.

The urban-suburban style of life displayed by the upper echelon of the factory personnel contrasts sharply with that pursued by ranking members of the native community. Rebhausen's social structure is very homogeneous, differentiated horizontally along a modal personality continuum, rather than vertically according to a vocational hierarchy. Since most families own some *Rebland* [vineyards] and engage in *Weinbau* on at least a part-time basis, practically every Rebhausen male is a farmer, in a cultural sense. The subsistence level of life and the recurring economic crises have operated to create and maintain a narrow range of individual wealth and to invest in the ownership of land a value of primary significance. The struggle for existence has required natives to return their income to the land. The use of

---

[3] The housing development site includes a beautiful new swimming pool which the younger generation of natives enjoy as much as factory personnel; but the new tennis courts, built by a factory-sponsored, private club, is to the older generation of natives an incomprehensible use of money and land.

profit for personal consumption, for example in home renovation, was a rare event prior to the establishment of the factory. The conspicuous display of wealth has been considered deviant behavior. To a stranger walking the streets of Rebhausen and visiting in the homes there is little evidence that one individual is more prosperous than another. Only in the past few years have signs of accumulated wealth begun to appear, in the purchase of cars and the renovation of homes.

Vocational classification, then, is no criterion for earning and achieving leadership roles in the community. Until recently, most members of the *Gemeinderat* have been elderly farmers. Leadership in the various social and recreational organizations and in the churches has followed a similar pattern. Leadership has been earned by individuals who work hard, are successful in their farming operations, get along well with their neighbors, are regular participants in the major activities of village life, and take good care of their families. An additional criterion for election to the *Gemeinderat* aside from a willingness to run, is membership in the Evangelical Church. (Catholics are usually able to elect one of their confession only if there is just one Catholic running.) Although factory personnel, in some instances, expressed a romantic love of the land, they ranked the life of the farmer low on their hierarchy of vocational interests. Consequently, Rebhausen natives are confronted with a social presence and force whose vocational value system is almost the inverse of their own. Vocational patterns and interests, therefore, have provided no avenues of contact between the two groups; rather they have operated to extend and maintain social distance and cultural alienation.

Political institutions have offered some opportunities for contacts, but at a very formal level and within the framework of a struggle for political power. From the very beginning, factory executives considered it important to be represented in the *Gemeinderat*—a necessary development, they felt, to further the best interests of the factory operation and of factory personnel. In the election of 1961, a foreman had been elected on the Social Democratic ticket. He had not received as many votes as several native candidates who failed to win seats, but the system of proportional representation, geared to encourage party affiliation and party growth, resulted in his being assigned the last of five seats up for election. In a *Gemeinderat* election when, for example, five seats are at stake, the voter has five votes to cast. He may distribute these among five candidates or give one candidate a maximum of three votes. Candidates must run under some kind of party designation. Winners are determined on the basis of total votes cast for each party list. Most of the native candidates ran as members of an independent party organized specifically for the election. Several natives ran as members of the Christian Democratic Union, a national party. Because of the system of proportional representation, one member of this party also won a *Gemeinderat* seat. Since the Social Democratic Party is by tradition and reputation a party of industrial workers, its appearance in the political life of the village constitutes another alien element which the factory is introducing.

There have been few informal social contacts between the two groups. When the factory became a reality, natives assumed that the new residents would begin immediately to participate in the traditional social and recreational activities. The mayor had expressed the same expectation. But, with the exception of the *Turnverein* (the gymnastic club in which the primary activities do not have any native-oriented cultural content), there have been few recruits. The traditional organizations appear to have little appeal to the newcomers. One migrant remarked that he had tried the *Gesangverein* but had found it difficult to sing enthusiastically the endless songs in praise of the Engelskrone. It wasn't *his* birthplace. Thus, those social contacts that develop tend to be structured by institutions—for example, parent meetings at the school. A few channels for more informal social contacts are developing, but these, significantly enough, are located more within the cultural milieu of the migrants than within the milieu of the natives—that is, bowling instead of the *Gesangverein*.

The pattern of extremely limited interaction between the two groups has nurtured the latent suspicion with which many natives view the influx of newcomers. The absence of productive contacts in the early years and the feedback from children (who in the school have had to confront a new, more aggressive kind of classmate) have led natives to feel that many of the newcomers view the village with some disdain. The native style of life includes few provisions for coping socially with strangers. The pattern of human relationships among natives is characterized by friendliness, based on a commitment to the traditional way of life. It can function to incorporate newcomers only if the latter exercise initiative and demonstrate interest in the village culture. Even then the probationary period can be long and uncertain. Nevertheless, those few factory personnel who set out to cultivate the friendship and trust of natives expressed satisfaction with the friendly response.

The village treasurer, a popular and congenial native, expressed these thoughts about the problem.

Before the factory, everyone in Rebhausen knew each other. Now that so many live here that's almost impossible. And then there's the influence of the city. Waldstadt is spreading out what with so many cars and all. People who move here come from cities like Berlin or Frankfurt or out of North Germany. They're not so inclined to be a part of village life. So Rebhausen is going to be more like a city. People will pass on the street and not know each other. It didn't use to be that way—when you'd walk down the street it was always, *"Horch einmal, wie gehts, was machst du?"* [Hullo there, how's it going, what are you doing?]. I mean the personal part of life in Rebhausen is disappearing.

Then, too, there's a difference between the North German and the South German. The South German is, well, more even-tempered, more sociable or good natured, more deliberate and cautious in the way he does things. The North German, on the other hand, is more active and energetic, speaks rapidly and with assurance—what you don't find so much in this part of the country.

That's all right of course. People are different. But the trouble is the newcomers to Rebhausen aren't so interested in the village. The best proof is the last town meeting. No one from the factory housing was there. They don't try to make contact with the village. The whole community was invited, and people came who were new to the village—those who through marriage have come here to live. But no one from the factory. They live their own lives. Certainly no one was opposed to their coming. I mean it isn't so that, if they had come, some one would have said, "What are you doing here?" It would please us if they would show interest. But they're of the opinion that *"dass ist ein Kuhdorf hinter dem Mond daheim"* [a hick town back in the sticks].

That kind of attitude is reflected in the school too. It's kind of taken for granted that the home town children are a little slower—and those from the city more outspoken and self-assured. I wouldn't say they're smarter. It's just that, well it's a matter of a different way of life.

Einheimische [natives] and *Zugezogene* [newcomers] are realistic enough to understand that the process of amalgamation will be a long, slow one. Natives no longer hold high expectations for newcomer participation in traditional activities. They speak more in terms of change over a generation. There is the conviction on the part of natives that their children will grow up to experience a more harmonious relationship with the inhabitants of the housing development and that Rebhausen will eventually be, in a cultural sense, one village. Parents also appear to view the school as the primary instrument of cultural synthesis. But this perspective has a forced quality to it, growing out of the feeling that such synthesis will take place at the expense of the traditional culture.

This chapter has described the economic base of community life, delineated the nature and extent of economic change and shown that, in spite of the benefits the factory has brought, the social ramifications are characterized by a deeply felt dissonance with which natives can not easily cope. The chapter has also provided a background against which to assess the appropriateness of education in Rebhausen. The question is for whom and for what purpose? Factory parents are quick to insist on a modern, urban-oriented educational program. Native parents want their children to be able to function successfully in a world of change, but subsequent chapters will show that the school life most satisfying to them and which is in fact operative is that which maintains and reinforces the traditional village culture.

Chapter 2 is concerned with preparatory institutions—with the socialization process as it proceeds in the home, the nursery, and the kindergarten. The material presented is necessarily limited in scope but representative of the milieu of native and factory families—and of those experiences most relevant to the demands of school life. The chapter begins with a sample of school life, the first month for first graders—a vantage point from which the socialization process and family life can be viewed.

2 / The school: preparatory institutions

FOUR WEEKS OF SCHOOL: A SAMPLE

THERE WAS AT FIRST no visible evidence that the opening day of school in late April had disturbed the village routine. It had rained early in the morning, and a gray dampness was enveloping Rebhausen in a drab, uninteresting atmosphere. But, by mid-morning, there was unusual movement in the streets. Young children, clinging tightly to their mothers, were being patiently shepherded to the elementary school in the center of town. A few arrived in cars, one was perched behind his mother on a tractor, but most of them walked.

School had already begun for the other grades. The three-story, gray stucco building with the Byzantine-like roof was noisy with the sound of teachers' and children's voices. Two classrooms were empty, reserved for the first graders when they had completed preparatory meetings. But the beginners hardly knew the rooms existed. They appeared preoccupied with the single, immediate event which engaged them. Furthermore, they literally had their hands full, each with a *Tüte*— a large, brightly colored, conically shaped cardboard container—crammed with candy, cookies, and useful articles and presented to them by their parents that morning.

The crowd of mothers and children collected at the *Turnhalle*. They were greeted by Rektor Doering—the genial, hefty, and balding young principal—and by the two first grade teachers—Frau Schenke and Frau Boettcher, attractive, young wives of Rebhausen teachers. When the group was seated, Herr Doering introduced the two teachers, commented on the significance of the day, joked with the children, and issued two emphatic warnings: 1) Parents should cooperate with the school in helping the children to learn quickly the basic traffic rules; and 2) they should be adamant in teaching their children not to get into cars with strangers.

He elaborated on the warnings and then moved to a discussion of class organization. The two classes were not divided strictly according to residence, he announced, as had traditionally been the case, with Oberdorf children in one section and "Rebhausen" children in the other. The division had always placed the factory children in the Rebhausen section. Since they were part of the total community, Herr Doering observed, he had split the factory housing development into two groups and assigned each to a different section. The meeting ended with the presentation of a small *Tüte* to each child. Herr Lamm, the owner of the local variety store, was the donor.

For the first graders the process of closure had begun in February. Early in the month the weekly community bulletin announced an evening meeting with the subject, "Is our child ready for school?" Rektor Doering presided and discussed characteristics of school readiness and touched in particular on school-readiness tests. He emphasized that they were routine and designed to help school officials make intelligent choices. He urged parents not to try to prepare the child for the tests, by anticipating the questions and forcing the child to practice on them. A misplaced child, the principal insisted, was a disfavor to all concerned.

Two weeks later the Rektor had an opportunity to find out if the parents had taken him seriously. School registration and examinations were scheduled for a day in late February. Parents and children came in small groups throughout the day. They reported to Herr Doering's office, registered, and moved from there to the faculty room where a public health nurse was set up to weigh, measure and give each child a T.B. test. The first real obstacle was a school readiness test.

A classroom had been set up for the test. Herr Schenke, the seventh grade teacher, gave the first part. As he called out numbers a child had to select the correct number from a collection of building blocks. Frau Boettcher administered the written part: "writing" a letter (a test of their ability to scratch down some lines with some kind of order), copying a three-word sentence, drawing replicates of four simple forms, reproducing a series of dots, and drawing a figure of a man and a tree. The atmosphere in the room was casual; about four children were there at a time, working on different parts of the test. Teachers wandered in and talked about the results. Herr Schenke worked to put each child at ease, with comments and questions, and also tried to discover if any of them had been practicing at home. One boy reported proudly that he had but that his father had forgotten to teach him how to draw a tree.

Of the 78 registering, 12 were refused admission; in the previous year 6 of 70 had been held back. Admission policies create a certain anxiety, although it was Herr Doering's experience that parents this year were more cooperative and understanding, due, he felt, to the increasing number of children whose parents (mainly factory personnel) are already planning on higher education. They want their children ready for the struggle and are more willing to postpone school entrance to enhance this aspiration. For the farmer who has traditionally expected his children (at least the son) to adopt his occupation and who is now facing a serious labor shortage, there is a strong vested interest in having his children proceed through school in the minimum length of time. If the mother works—at farming or in the factory—a year's postponement can be especially disconcerting.

The first day of class began after lunch. A light rain was falling, but children (and mothers along for one more day of moral support) stood quietly and expectantly outside, waiting to be called in. Finally the two teachers appeared, instructed their respective classes to come in, and told the mothers to come back in two hours. In Frau Boettcher's room the children marched up to the front and got their name tags. A few of the smaller children were placed in the front seats; most of them could sit with their friends. When they were settled, she asked them to read their names and describe the picture on the tags. One girl started to speak. "Schön melden" [Raise your hand first], Frau Boettcher instructed her. Others caught on and hands went up. They all had a chance to introduce themselves. Then she called them up front. They formed a circle, sang a song about a rabbit, and then were told to hop back to their seats. They did with great glee and noise. A story followed. Frau Boettcher read well; the children were quiet. She stopped in the middle and asked a question about the story. The chorus of replies was loud but ragged so she tuned them in again:

"Now, altogether—where did the rabbit hide?"

"Under the house!"

That was better. She went on to other questions. A girl raised her hand, was called on and started to answer. Frau Boettcher interrupted and told her to stand up by her desk when she was reciting. Some of the children already knew that; some remembered halfway through a recitation and suddenly jumped up. The teacher finished the story and told the class to get out their slates, pencils, and erasers (a damp sponge to clean, a small cloth to dry). She walked down the aisle to inspect their equipment, reminded them always to keep a *"schöne, saubere Tafel"* [a nice, clean slate], and told them how damp to keep the sponge.

She asked more questions about the story. Some of the children answered without out bothering to stand up but Frau Boettcher did not seem to mind. They talked about the story and she told them to draw a picture of an animal in it. She walked down the aisle, inspecting their work. *"Die Nase hoch"* [Keep your nose up], she instructed one boy who had his head buried in his drawing. Frau Boettcher placed a finger under his nose and gently lifted his head up. The questioning continued. One boy was not paying attention. *"Klaus schläft schon ein"* [Klaus is falling asleep], Frau Boettcher announced to the class. They all laughed.

The time came for a break in the routine. She told them to stand up, shake their fingers and hands, and clap in unison. They sat down and continued drawing. Finally Frau Boettcher told them to stop, clean the slates, and put them neatly away. She urged them to hurry and see who was first and last. The winner and loser were announced, the class was dismissed for a five-minute recess, and she led them outside. Another teacher had playground duty, so Frau Boettcher and I remained in the hall talking with the teachers who were gathered there.

At the end of the recess Herr Greiner, who had the duty, climbed the steps facing the playground and from the top clapped his hands. The children formed two lines at the bottom of the steps, lining up by classes. The first graders were at the front, staring wide-eyed at Herr Greiner. When the lines were formed, he signaled them to come in. The lines broke up inside the door as the children headed for separate classrooms. The first graders were still a little confused, but Frau Boettcher directed them back to the classroom. We waited outside until all the children were in the room and seated. Then we went in. One or two stood up; a few others started to rise, slowly and hesitantly. She told them to stand up when anyone entered the room.

It was near the end of the day. She asked the children if they had ever heard of homework. No one answered, so she explained it. She told them there would be none on the first day but that it would certainly please her if they wanted to draw some kind of picture about the story. Then she called the class up front. They formed a circle with one child in the middle. He was to walk around the inside and pick out someone to take his place. He pointed; the other child moved to the center. They stood facing each other, bowed or curtsied, and changed places. They were shy and could not decide whom to pick—and they bowed or curtsied in a stiff, self-conscious manner. She had to keep telling them to pick someone and to bow correctly. Sometimes it went very well, with the movement of a minuet.

They made progress, so she sent them back to their seats to clean up. They pulled out their satchels and began packing the notebooks and equipment they had already accumulated. When they were ready, they stood by their desks and Frau Boettcher announced who was first and last. Then she taught them a song:

Schule ist aus   [School is out
Nach Haus,   We're going home,
Nach Haus.   We're going home.]

They sang loudly and cheerfully and then she recited a prayer for them. Some of them already knew it from kindergarten. She worked on the first few lines with the others; then they all said it, heads bowed, eyes closed, hands folded in front. When they were through, they finished packing their satchels and hoisted them up on their backs. There was a rush toward the door but she stopped them.

"Don't forget to say good-by," she reminded them.

The response was immediate. *"Auf Wiedersehen, Frau Boettcher,"* already in the slow, measured rhythm they would use for eight years.

The first month was an impressive introduction to a pattern of school life sharply characterized by structure and order. From an institutional point of view, the first grader experienced a process of social incorporation which not only had a central focus on authority but which also allowed few alternatives or deviations. The incorporation process was experienced directly—particularly through the style and intensity of discipline imposed by the teacher and indirectly through, for example, academic channels of expression which imposed minimal possibilities for freely chosen responses.

The use of language was especially significant. Pupils were encouraged to render thought patterns, simple emotional reactions, ideas about proper conduct in the classroom, and ideas about basic social and personal relationships with family members and peers, in a mode of expression that had literally a poetic form and rhythm. More attention was given to an appropriate verbal rendition of this form and rhythm than to a free, relatively unstructured exploration of its content. How a pupil answered a question was important but isolated from the social and interpersonal context of the classroom. The emphasis on the use of the voice appeared to turn the pupil in on himself, away from an awareness of the relationship of what he said to what other pupils thought and said.

Poetry was an instrument of religious expression. The first opening prayer they learned was:

Mit Gott fang an,	[Begin with God,
Mit Gott hör auf,	End with God,
Dass is der schönste Lebenslauf.	That's the best way to live.]

It was an instrument of instruction, for example, in proper traffic safety rules. They were taught in the first week the following poem.

Links die Nase,	[Look left,
Rechts die Nase,	Look right,
Kommst du sicher über die Strasse.	You'll come safely across the street.]

It was an instrument of discipline. Frau Boettcher started on the second day teaching them to pay attention and to avoid whispering and pointless talking with their classmates. She told them to remember:

Eins, zwei, drei,	[One, two, three,
Schwätzen ist vorbei.	Be as quiet as can be.]

Poetry was invoked to furnish the pupil a mode of expressing family love. In preparation for Mother's Day, Frau Boettcher proposed that they give flowers and, when presenting them, recite the following poem:

Liebe Mutter nimm als Gabe	[Mother dear, accept as a gift
Dieses Blumenssträuchen an,	This bouquet of flowers,
Es ist alles was ich habe,	It's all that I have,
Alles was ich schenken kann.	All that I can give you.]

There were poems and songs for every occasion. A streak of rainy weather produced the following incantation.

Rinken, ranken Rosenschein,	[Happy sun, shine on us.]
Liebe Sonne kommt herein.	

They learned to recite with an enthusiasm and an expressiveness that was, to a stranger, touching and entertaining. If it was not poetry they had to recite but simply the answer to a question, they were, nevertheless, led to experience the expediency of acceptable verbal expression. If the answer required only a few words, Frau Boettcher taught them to use complete sentences. If the answer was inaudible, she often sent them to the back of the room to try again and to make sure the whole room heard clearly.

Frau Boettcher was not the stereotype of a schoolteacher. Young, vivacious, cheerful, she created a friendly classroom atmosphere and evoked from the children a noticeable personal affection. But as an adult and a teacher she imposed on classroom life a firm, unbending structure of authority and carefully patterned behavior. The children learned appropriate physical responses within a few weeks. The second day they were exposed to an exercise in standing up and greeting any adult who entered the room. After recess, when the children were seated, Frau Boettcher entered the room, stood at the door, and reminded them of the social obligation. Then she withdrew, shut the door, waited a few seconds, and entered a second time. They were ready. When, on the third day, a teacher entered with a message, the class performed admirably, but forgot the salutation. So they all practiced together, *"Auf Wiedersehen, Frau Schenke."* Social obligations of this kind had to be carefully related to age groupings. The first time a pupil, a fifth grader, entered the room, the class was thrown into confusion. Some stood up promptly, some remained seated, others hovered halfway between, wondering which direction to choose. After several such instances she helped them solve their dilemma. But there were always a few who found the appearance of an overgrown eighth grader an insoluble problem.

They learned quickly to stand up to recite; it became an automatic response— or almost automatic. There were exceptions, never clearly defined and rather unpredictable. A pupil might start his answer on the way up and finish it in a rather undecided position. Sometimes Frau Boettcher ignored the halfhearted effort; sometimes she made him stand up properly and repeat the answer. But there were no exceptions at the end of the day when the children said good-by. They did not have to shake hands but when they chose to, out of a sense of duty or a feeling of attachment, the boys were to bow and the girls to curtsy. If the body movement was not emphatic enough, they were kidded and told to try again.

Appropriate relationships with adults was a basic social and educational objective to which first graders were effectively sensitized. Physical cleanliness was another. Rules for acceptable cleanliness were not just identified within the context of a good individual health and hygiene program. They were pronounced, implemented, and reinforced through teacher admonition and appeal to group disapproval. The rules were simple: clean hands, face, fingernails, and handkerchief. Shoes were supposed to be polished; that had been the tradition, but there appeared to be less concern about it now.

The first inspection was on the sixth day, as the children were about to leave. Frau Boettcher suddenly told them to put their hands palms down on the desks— and then she started down the aisles, scattering comments as she went.

"Max, your fingernails look like a mourning band. See how clean Hans' are! Rudolph, don't your parents have any water at home, any soap, faucets, towels— anything to get your hands clean? Better look out." The next day, just before drawing, she inspected again, this time handkerchiefs too. They held them up high; she looked around the room and told some of them to put the handkerchiefs back into their pockets quickly—they were too repulsive. Then she started down the aisle inspecting their hands. Rudolph had not done his homework. She exploded. "You look like a little pig!" She grabbed him by the hands, pulled him out of his seat, and marched him down the aisle with his hands spread out in front. She told the children she didn't want to see anything that bad again, as the two of them disappeared through the door to the washroom.

Frau Boettcher meant for the handkerchiefs to be used. Heinrich was sitting in the back of the room one day sniffing rather loudly. Frau Boettcher was at the blackboard. *"Wer hat die musikalische Nase?"* [Who has the musical nose?] No one answered. She asked again. Heinrich stopped sniffing.

There were other rules and responsibilities which children had to learn and accept if they were to survive the academic program. Use of the slate required a special pencil, a sponge, a cloth, and above all, a particular body position. The slate was to be placed directly in front, properly squared off with the desk, feet squarely in front, legs together, left arm folded in front between the body and the slate and resting on the desk. It was not a posture program that she had worked out. The county school inspector had simply decreed that it was the best posture for writing—so that was the way she did it. This they learned on the third day, when reading and writing began. The first page in their reader had a picture of a little boy painting. Frau Boettcher wrote on the board, "Hans paints." Then she told them to write the word Hans in the air with their finger, then on the desk, and finally on the slate.

By the fourth day a routine had developed which the children could become used to—so long as they could remember when school started each day. It varied during the week, from 7:30 A.M. to 10:00 A.M., depending on what was scheduled. There were always reading and writing and practically always homework—for example, write the word Hans five time on the slate. There was always arithmetic. Counting objects drawn on the blackboard was a beginning: "Ein Ringlein und ein Ringlein sind zwei Ringlein," [One ring and one ring are two rings.] They counted singly, in pairs, and in unison. They came to the blackboard to practice, but there was little time to ponder an answer. *"Schnell, schnell"* [fast, fast], was the tempo.

There were drawing, singing, storytelling, games. The children came to school prepared to recite or soon learned it was central to their success and standing with the teacher. When the opportunity to recite involved something special, for example, going to the front of the room to use the flannel board, the response was almost deafening. Hands waved frantically, fingers snapped loudly, voices cried plaintively, *"ich, ich, ich."* Even a response to a routine question was invariably excited.

The children learned to experience praise and censure before the entire class. If their slate work was especially good, Frau Boettcher held up examples for the whole class to see. She displayed their drawings and praised other aspects of their work. She was spontaneous and enthusiastic in her expression of affection. If they were slow in their work, they heard about it! "Rudolph talks a lot but doesn't get much done. Hans is asleep again." If there was a disturbance, she warned the culprits, spoke sharply to them, and in some instances tugged at the hair and twisted ears. Discipline was in most cases gentle but swift and firm.

The State Constitution affirms the right of parents to a cooperative role in school affairs, and the Ministry of Education had implemented this provision with a communique making mandatory the organization of a parent's council. Consequently, within a month after the opening of school, meetings were scheduled by all teachers. First grade parents gathered in their children's classroom. Twenty were present for Frau Boettcher's meeting, five men and fifteen women, representing about 50 percent of the children in the class. She had some opening remarks prepared and a list of suggestions she hoped the parents would follow:

1. Inspect your children's hands and fingernails in the morning. They can get dirty on the way to school, but some of them come with what appears to be a three-day accumulation.
2. Inspect their satchels and make them clean out the junk that accumulates.
3. Don't tell them what the letters are when they make a mistake in their writing. They aren't ready to learn the names of the letters. Just tell them when they have made a mistake.
4. Don't let them start to school too early. They are not supposed to be here earlier than ten minutes before the bell.
5. Don't give them too big a *Vesper* [mid-morning snack]. They don't have time to eat it.
6. Don't believe everything they claim I have told them.
7. Don't take your children shopping during school hours. It is not allowed. Attendance at a wedding or a funeral is permissible so long as it is a close relative, but, please, not for a sixth cousin.

She went on to discuss her hopes for the year and to make suggestions about school supplies that parents would be buying—and then there were questions.

1. Why does school have to begin so early (7:30 A.M.)?
   Answer: Overcrowded conditions. We might be able to improve the schedule when the new building is completed.
2. Why must they come home so late at noon (12:15 P.M.)?
   Answer: Same problem—the schedule.
3. When will the student traffic patrol leaders be operating?
   Answer: As soon as the new building is ready. Right now, since classes have already begun up there, there is much confusion and the patrol leaders are needed.
4. Why don't you give 1's (the equivalent of A's)?
   Answer: They don't belong at this level. If children become accustomed to 1's now, the grade won't mean as much to them in the upper grades. Anyway, you shouldn't put too much pressure on them about grades.

The talk about grades went on and then Frau Boettcher reminded them they were there to elect two individuals to serve as chairman and co-chairman of their own first grade group and as representatives of the group to the parents' council. She asked for nominations. Four men and two women were nominated. The balloting was simple. It ought to be, observed Frau Boettcher; membership on the council did not require much time, and there was seldom anything unpleasant to be concerned with—which was the purpose of the council in the first place. Herr Kranz, a middle-aged businessman, native and a member of the village council, was elected chairman. Frau Doering, wife of the principal and a first grade mother, was elected co-chairman. The meeting broke up and parents started home, talking about their children and homework, the teachers, their own school experiences.

THE FAMILY

Patterns of child rearing in Rebhausen are not markedly different among factory and native families. Hospital facilities in Waldstadt have for years been available to Rebhausen mothers—and made more accessible between the two world wars through the improvement of the road system. Since that time most babies have been born in Waldstadt hospitals.

A birth is first really celebrated six weeks later when the baby is baptized. Up to the recent decade, baptism had been, for practical reasons, as early as two weeks following the birth. Rebhausen traditions required that a mother should not leave the house and go back to work in the fields until she had appeared in church with the child and had it baptized. So she usually came as soon as she could. Pfarrer Riedel, the Evangelical minister, had identified a good many traditions governing female conduct in church affairs which he hoped to be able to change. This was one of them. One day in a church meeting, he insisted that the tradition did not make sense—that a mother should be able to come to church when she was ready to and arrange the baptism later. Since the practice was beginning to die out, his admonition was acceded to.

Baptism takes place at the end of the regular Sunday service and is followed by a celebration dinner to which close relatives and godparents are invited. The godfather [*Pate*] and godmother [*Patin*] are chosen before the birth, almost always from among relatives, and one or more of each sex. Uncles and aunts (if possible young and unmarried) from both sides of the family have priority, followed by cousins, distant relatives, and long-time family friends. The godparent-godchild relationship is maintained until the latter marries; its initiation creates a matrix of interlocking relationships and obligations which gives structure and reinforcement to the extended family system, especially the outer edges where obligations are not as clearly defined. The invitation is seldom refused; approbation would be severe.

Ideally, godparents are to exercise a beneficent influence on the moral and spiritual development of the child. They are extensions of the parental influence, enlarging and reinforcing what is experienced in the home. There is no evidence that a godparent is by virtue of the selection invested with disciplinary responsibilities or authority. However, there is a moral, if not a legal, obligation to take over the care of a godchild should something disastrous happen to both parents. Practically speaking, the real obligations set up by the act of selection are financial. Each year at Christmas, Easter, and birthdays, children pay special visits to their godparents who are ready with presents. This practice continues in Evangelical families until children are confirmed at the end of the eighth grade and in Catholic families until communion in the ninth year. From this point on, no gifts are expected until the godchild's wedding.

In past generations the relationship was an uncomplicated social mechanism. The village was poor; the financial obligation laid upon any godparent was not drastic. There was not much to give, and the simple gift, a symbol of love and attachment, was always reinforced by continuous personal interaction—made possible by residential and work patterns. The development of a relatively affluent, urban, and mobile style of life complicated the obligation. Personal interaction has decreased, and the almost limitless variety of price and kind of toy has loaded the choice of gifts with a commercial value. Herr Langenbeck, a native, white-collar worker in the factory, complained that making a wise choice was almost impossible. A godparent had to avoid a cheap gift for fear that the godchild's parents, usually a brother or sister, would decide the proper amount of interest was not being shown. He had to anticipate the quality of gifts his children would receive. So the gifts tended to be too expensive; the ones his children received at Christmas were too complicated. He had to put them away until the children were older. He summed up his feelings this way: *"Paten sein ist eine Ehr' aber es macht den Geldbeutel leer,"* [Being a godfather is an honor but it's hard on the pocketbook.]

The six-week-old baby who is baptized is in the process of being weaned. Breast feeding in previous generations continued for as long as a year; if the mother's supply of milk dried up, a bottle was used until the child was old enough to sit at the table. Mother's milk is still, in the village, valued as the most natural and healthful food supply in the early months, and wet nurses are highly valued in nearby hospitals. There is the general conviction that the older generations are healthier because they were breast-fed longer. But Rebhausen mothers are busy and an increasing number of them are working, so there is a widespread use of baby foods in the early months.

Given normal physical growth, early weaning accelerates the socialization process by exposing the growing child, almost as soon as it is physically possible, to the father's role. In spite of the long hours a father may spend at work, in the fields, or in the factory, he consistently exercises a powerful influence on the adjustment of growing children to the normal routine of the home, especially behavior at the table, and on the child's outside social interests. Frau Becker, forty-one years old, recalled these aspects of her early years:

> What I remember, first of all, is that in kindergarten we learned to sing and pray, and at home there was real respect for parents. Above all we had to obey. Often I feel that then a child had more—I won't say anxiety—real respect for his parents, more than our children—especially with regard to the father. He was more of a "Respektsperson" then. There wasn't so much of a comradely relationship. When the father said something, a child had to obey immediately and without being sullen about it. When a visitor came, we were expected to know in advance—while we were still very small children—that we weren't to talk at the table. After the meal with visitors we weren't to speak unless we were asked something.
>
> My father was really strict. Often when something went wrong among us children and we started quarreling he would spank us all and not bother to ask who had started the trouble. My mother wasn't so strict; she was kind of a reconciler. I think my mother didn't always agree with the way my father treated us, but, of course, she never gave any indication in his presence. But later it was possible to tell. She wasn't so demanding and raised us more freely.
>
> Maybe it was my father's own upbringing. Absolute obedience I guess was what he had had to learn. He had a hard youth and often told us about it—he had to get up early and go into the fields for green fodder and bring home a wagon full before school. His father didn't want to hear a thing about school —only work—that was all that counted.

I think our children grow up in a freer atmosphere. Parents aren't always so strict nowadays, and they don't always take every word at its face value. A child often says something without thinking; they don't concern themselves that it might sound impudent. I take those chances to tell my children that that is not permitted—that after all I am a mother and what they might say to their playmates they shouldn't say to their parents.

My father wouldn't bother to talk about it, if we said something that sounded impudent. Up would come his hand and we'd get a box on the ear. I can still remember an incident—I was already engaged and was 22 years old. I said something to my father which was certainly not meant to be impudent, but it must have struck him that way. I had hardly finished the sentence when he slapped me right in the face. That's the way it was, with my friends too. They were as afraid of their fathers as I was of mine.

The traditional, forceful role of the father is not as pronounced as it once was, and physical punishment is not as frequently used, but the change is tentative. Gottfried Henkel, a young auto mechanic with two small children, is representative of a generation which is experiencing conflict about traditional family mores.

When it comes to raising children I don't throw out the American system completely. From what I've heard and seen on television Americans are much freer in bringing up children—they give the kids more leeway. Of course, I've heard that it sometimes happens in an American family that a father has to wait an hour to use the telephone, because his kids have it tied up.

I don't know—I guess there is more than one way of doing things. My upbringing certainly wasn't strict, but that was because shortly after I was born my father went to war and was killed. My mother had to raise us three boys, and a mother can't be real strict with boys. But I think she did all right. If you look at all of us, I don't think you can notice that we have had no father when we were being brought up. And she did it with love. She never said, "You must, you better, or else you'll get a spanking." It was always, "You do that, please." I liked that way!

We talked about what he remembered from his early childhood, what his mother tried to teach him, what she felt was important.

The thing I can remember first is learning to pray, and I think that's what our children are beginning with. I don't think there is as much interest in the church as there once was, but a person ought to have a certain belief, and you have to start with little children.

Then, well, there are all the things kids have to learn—to develop what adults call "den guten Ton"—like being the first to express greetings when you pass an older person, helping older people carry packages, and things like that.

We could speak at the table but we had to eat everything served, and we learned to pray before and after the meal. She always told us never to go outside with dirty shoes. She kept reminding us that a person ought to give the impression that he was correctly and properly and cleanly brought up.

I asked him whether he thought he and his wife were raising their children the way the two of them had been brought up and if they were trying to teach their children the same basic values and attitudes.

> Pretty much so, I guess, but not like a lot of other people do today. For instance, we don't get upset if he comes in from play dirty. We know it's bound to happen. But some of our friends tell their boys they shouldn't get down on their knees when they play. That may be kind of an exception but as a general rule when kids go out to play they are supposed to come home fairly clean.
>
> We start in early teaching the children good table manners. Our boy who is five has known for a long time that he is to remain quiet at the table and not talk, and, of course, he must stay at the table until we are through. We want him to eat first. Then, if his plate is clean, he can tell us about what happened in kindergarten. He learned quickly. By the time he was a year and a half we could go out to eat without his doing something that would call attention to us.

The kind of behavior required of children at the table is not without its lighter moments. Herr Schinn, an unskilled worker at the factory, related that at a recent meal he sent his five-year-old to the cellar to refill the wine jug. The boy returned, sat down, and started to tell his father about something. Herr Schinn told him to be quiet and finish his meal. This exchange was repeated several times, until finally the boy managed to blurt out that the spigot on the wine cask was stuck and he couldn't close it.

Four parents of first graders.   At the parent's meeting Frau Boettcher gave me an opportunity to describe my interests in the first grade. After the meeting, a number of parents expressed a willingness to talk to me about their family life. From these contacts and others, I selected what I considered to be a representative group.

1. Günter Jaide is the father of three boys, ages seven and five years, and eight months. Both he and his wife were born and raised in Rebhausen. He graduated from the elementary school in 1947, attended a vocational school for three years, and graduated as a carpenter. For ten years he worked in Rebhausen and then spent two years in Munich driving an ambulance for the Red Cross. He wanted to stay there. The work was hard on his nerves but at the end of each day he said he felt good inside.

Ultimately he had to leave Munich and return to Rebhausen to take over his father's house. His father was too feeble to work. After five years of employment with a local construction company he became chief foreman. We gathered around the dining room table; Herr Jaide, a husky man with prematuring gray hair, heavy, thick eyebrows and deep-set, opaque blue eyes, sat at one end, Frau Jaide at the other end, and the two older boys opposite me on the sides. The children were allowed to draw in their notebooks while we talked. On several occasions Frau Jaide ventured a supportive remark, but Herr Jaide spoke most of the time.

> The most important thing to each children is obedience, then everything else comes easy. We love our children and make sure they know that, and we try to

teach them what the right things are by being good examples ourselves. We try to concentrate on basic things like manners, honesty, cooperation.

But kids aren't always going to do the right thing and then they have to be punished. Sometimes all I have to do is send them out of the room—tell them I don't want them to be around me if they are going to act that way. That works good. Sometimes though you have to be harder on them. I don't ever hit them on top of the head, but a slap on the cheek or the ear doesn't hurt. A spanking is good or twisting the ear or pulling the hair at the temple. Actually I don't have to punish them much. They know beforehand what they're supposed to do. They know, for example, if they come home with dirty shoes they'll be punished.

What Frau Boettcher said the other night at the parent's meeting wasn't so necessary—at least for any normal parent. Take a look at my kids' hands—they're clean. They know when they're through playing that they have to clean up. As for grades, well, the parent who kept wanting to know why Boettcher didn't use 1's, I know him. He's from the factory and figured he didn't need to send his kid to kindergarten so long. So she doesn't know enough religion, and he wants the teacher to give higher grades so that his kid will work harder. I don't think the 1 is so important. What is important is what a kid does and how much he wants to learn.

That makes kindergarten important. They get vauable religious training, but they also get a chance to play as much as they want to, so when they enter school they're ready to settle down and work.

We talked for about two hours. The children sat quietly, listening and drawing. The first grader had demonstrated in school a talent for drawing, and Frau Boettcher had commented on this to Jaide at the meeting. As we talked, he periodically checked his son's work and told him how to improve it.

2. Jacob Schneider is a refugee from Stettin, a graduate of a *Gymnasium* [College preparatory high school] and a *Wirtschaftshochschule* [commercial college]. He worked his way, after the war, to Hannover and found a job in an appliance concern. A friend there put him in contact with officials in the chemical factory. He came down to look over the opportunity and decided to move, attracted primarily by the natural surroundings. After six years in Rebhausen he has not regretted the move and is now an executive in the sales department. He is disturbed about the educational and cultural disadvantages. The school is not strong, and a person has to go to Waldstadt for dramatic and musical events. But the people in Rebhausen are very friendly, more so than in other parts of Germany he has known.

The interview began before dinner on a Sunday afternoon and continued into the late afternoon. Frau Schneider was busy most of the time with the meal. When she finally found time to come into the apartment living room, she sat quietly listening to us talk, entering into the conversation only in response to a question or remark directed at her by Schneider. The assessment of his daughter and their relationship to her is his.

Jutta has been a nervous child in these early years. Her mother had difficulty with the birth, and Jutta had to spend the first five months in the hospital. It may have had something to do with later difficulties. Her toilet training was slow; she didn't stay clean until she was over two and a half. Thumb sucking continued until she was four, not during the day but only at night after she went to bed. We tried everything but she didn't stop until one day we showed her what might happen to her teeth if she kept on. We didn't let her use a *Schnuller* [pacifier]; it's unsanitary, and people who give it to their kids are just lazy.

I suppose you could say that we have worked most on teaching her to be independent, to practice good rules of safety, and to understand that life is not all play—that it has to be mastered, that it has demands that have to be met. And we want her to behave properly. I've told her many times, "Benehme dich zu Hause als wenn du beim Kaiser bist." [Behave at home as if you were in the presence of the Kaiser.] We think this is important. We want her to use good table manners, not to eat food on the streets and to always curtsy and say good day to adults.

We punish her in a way that we think will do her the most good. Personally, I think the American way is too soft. We spank her when it seems necessary, but only on the rear end. I don't believe in slapping her or twisting her ear, but if she is impudent or not acting her age she knows she'll get a spanking.

Frau Boettcher is a good teacher. She is friendly but has a firm quality I like. I think though she might do more for the brighter kids. Higer grades might help. The pace of the class is influenced too much by the weaker kids and that's bad for the better students, especially when they get ready to enter a Gymnasium. The truth is, as compared with the city, the environment in the country is not very demanding or stimulating. In the city kids have to think and react faster—due to traffic—and they see enough different things to understand that life is not very simple. All that is not true with kids who grow up in the country. Still these kids here have close contact with nature and that's important too.

3. Fritz Langenbeck, a white-collar worker in the factory, was born and raised in Rebhausen. His father had been a mason, and after finishing the Rebhausen school Herr Langenbeck decided to become a mason. Shortly after finishing vocational school he broke his leg in an accident. Complications followed, he was in the hospital for over a year, and his leg became permanently stiff. Masonry was eliminated as a vocation, so he enrolled at a business school and started work in the factory. His wife graduated from a home economics school and worked for two years in a shoe factory. She was born and raised in a village near Rebhausen. They have two boys, ages seven and three, and occupy a three-room apartment in the factory housing development.

Their daily routine is typical of families in this housing area. Herr Langenbeck and his family are up at 6:30 A.M. School for the older boy begins at 7:30, and Herr Langenbeck has to be at the factory at 8:00. Their breakfast is minimal—for the parents, coffee and a piece of bread and butter, for the boys, a soupy porridge [*Brei*] which can be drunk or eaten. The boys can have a piece of bread when they have finished the porridge. Herr Langenbeck and Fritz, the older boy, always take a mid-morning lunch with them—usually a sandwich and fruit. After they have gone, Frau Langenbeck delivers the younger boy to the kindergarten and spends the morning cleaning the house and making the rounds of the shops for bread, staples, and meat.

The noon meal, hot and nourishing, is the important meal of the day. They have soup at least twice a week, a vegetable, salad, potatoes or noodles, and meat—usually pork—at least four times a week. Dessert is reserved for Sunday.

Kindergarten begins in the afternoon at 1:00 as does Herr Langenbeck's work. Fritz returns to school at 1:30 once or twice a week and is home again by 3:30. His younger brother at this age attends kindergarten only in the morning and so is home when he arrives. Fritz has to do his homework and straighten his room before he can go out to play; if he wastes time at his work Frau Langenbeck keeps him in for the afternoon. Herr Langenbeck arrives home—a walk of several blocks —at 5:00. The family eats a second *Vesper* [light meal] at around 6:00—usually bread, cold meat and cheese, and for the parents beer or wine. They try to have the boys in bed by 7:00, but they have had to compromise. Both of them go to bed then, but, when Jurgen is asleep Fritz is allowed to get up and spend an extra half hour in the living room—if he does his homework.

The boys have to keep their rooms straight, and Fritz has to dry the dishes during the week. On the weekends Herr Langenbeck takes over this job—he says he does it partly to show Fritz that it is an acceptable chore for a man to perform when there are no girls in the family. Fritz is also required to help out with other household duties. The one chore that regularly takes him out of the apartment is getting the milk at night. Pasteruized milk can be purchased in Rebhausen, but fresh milk is more popular and healthful according to many residents. Most people buy their milk, therefore, either at the milk station or directly from farmers. The village scene early in the evening is one of numerous children of all ages moving through the streets. Fritz has been getting the milk since he was four years old.

The Langenbecks say Fritz is a boy who cries easily, so they do not punish him too severely. They seldom spank him or use a stick. Frau Langenbeck finds that a sharp word is usually enough. If that doesn't work, they make him stay in his room part of the day. Jurgen is harder to discipline; sharp words, a spanking, and in five minutes, he is engaged in the same unacceptable behavior. So Frau Langenbeck uses a stick across the fingers or at least threatens him with a beating. That works but what she finds most effective is to reject him—tell him that he has been so bad that she does not want to have anything to do with him. This makes him anxious, she finds, and he improves.

Rewards that the two boys might expect or hope for are generally tied in with trips the parents make to Waldstadt. They usually go every Saturday morning to shop for what they cannot or do not want to purchase in Rebhausen. Fritz is given the key to the apartment, should they not make it home until after school is out—or arrangements are made for him to eat the noon meal with his grandmother. They remind the boys, during the week, of the Waldstadt trip, a device which helps to improve their behavior.

Herr Langenbeck described other trips they made, which created expectations and uncertainties in the minds of the boys, especially Fritz.

Since Fritz reached five we have felt free to go out some evenings. On Sunday night we often go to Waldstadt to a movie, a coffee shop, or just to window shop. We're gone about three hours. We've told the boys that we have to go out once in a while, and we tell Fritz that he is growing up and can take care of his little brother. When we started doing this Fritz was anxious and worried. My wife had told him once that if he didn't improve his conduct he might get a stepmother in place of her. I guess when we first went out, he thought she was never coming back.

We don't tell the Veldmanns down below us when we go out. We just lock the door from the outside, hang the key over the door and have an understanding with the Veldmanns that if there is any prolonged crying they will investigate. If the crying is short, they can figure out that we are up there. Of course, we warn the boys never to answer the doorbell when we aren't there. It seems to work out all right. Some parents start going out and leaving their kids alone when the oldest one is only four, but that's a little young.

The Langenbecks were pleased with Fritz's progress in school, liked Frau Boettcher, and had no complaints about the schedule, grading, or any other aspect of school life.

4. Frau Wetzel is the wife of a truck driver who contracts out to construction companies. They have three children, the youngest of whom is beginning the first grade. Herr Wetzel is a native of Rebhausen; she is from Rottenheim, a predominantly Catholic village in the vicinity. They are both Catholic. The interview took place in their home on a weekday afternoon. It was one of few instances in which the mother alone was present to answer my questions. Herr Wetzel had long working hours, came home late at night and was, in addition, markedly reserved. His wife indicated that an afternoon meeting would be preferable. The interview was an exception to the pattern of interchange between Rebhausen parents and me. Husbands generally maintained the initiative in our conversations about children, even children of preschool age.

I asked Frau Wetzel what she expected of the children and how she disciplined them.

They don't generally have chores before they go to school—only when they come home and have left their room in a mess—then I leave it that way and make them clean it up. Otherwise only the girl helps me sweep and do a few household jobs. I get the others to run errands and help me now and then with the dishes. But I don't make them because then they wouldn't do it glady. If I tell them they may help, or if I offer them something for it, then they do it more willingly.

I find that one has to be very strict today with the children. I've found that out by observing young people today—and my man always says that the teachers and ministers aren't strict enough. You know what happens then—the children lose respect for their parents. I don't know how I can say it, but when children aren't afraid of the teacher—I mean they shouldn't have fear—but anyway they don't have real respect any longer. When they don't, they don't behave as well at home!

My man has very little to do with bringing up the kids. He can't, he says, spend his only free day spanking the kids. When I tell him that they didn't behave he just says, "That's your business. I can't just go in there at night when they're in bed and start beating them on the ass." But the children behave better when he is at home. I think they're a little afraid of him.

The Wetzels do not go out at night together, not since they have had children. They did once and left the children home alone in bed asleep. There was a silver wedding anniversary celebration in a local restaurant, a few blocks away. When they returned home after midnight, all the lights were on and the children were awake. They had awakened earlier and could not find their parents. So now, when she wants to see a movie, he stays home, and she is there when he goes bowling. Neighborhood relations, as well as the safety of the children, concern them. They do not want the children, in their absence, to create a disturbance that would rouse the neighbors. In this respect they were impressed by an incident in the neighborhood. The parents had left after the children were asleep. The young daughter woke up, found the parents absent, and grew hysterical, standing on the doorstep yelling and crying. An older brother, eleven years, was sleeping through it all. Neighbors had to go into the house and wake the brother.

THE NURSERY

Typically, Rebhausen children's first contact with an organized program of instruction and play begins at age three or four when they enter kindergarten. But, if circumstances make it desirable or necessary, parents can bring their offspring to the village nursery, as early as six weeks after birth. Until 1962, the nursery had been run by the churches and administered in conjunction with the kindergartens. The arrangemnt was convenient; parents with preschool children could deposit them all at one place. Total enrollment then was between fifty and sixty children. After 1962, when the state imposed stricter health and sanitation regulations, the churches found they could not afford to support the nurseries. The community took them over and moved them into one building—the back portion of a long-defunct cigar factory, the front of which is being used by the chemical factory as a dormitory for foreign workers. Enrollment is now between twenty and twenty-five.

It is not difficult to find the building which houses the nursery. Faded but still visible on the front of the building is *Zigarrenfabrik*, [Cigar Factory] and on a warm day there are always a few Turkish workers lounging at the windows or in the small front yard, talking in their native tongue, smoking, and it appears, idly engaged in girl-watching. When I first visited the nursery it was a hot day. The door at the top of three steep steps was wide open but barred by a play pen which was occupied, but which also served as a gate to keep the children in. Behind the play pen were a conglomeration of children and babies, strapped in chairs, playing in pens, staggering unsteadily around the room. In the middle of the play area, strung out in a ragged column, were seven children, perched on pots. They were quiet, contented, and apparently waiting for something to happen.

The daily routine begins before lunch. The children are delivered between 11:00 A.M. and noon, and since they are scheduled shortly for a nap, toilet training begins immediately. After this session they are given a snack, allowed to play for a few minutes, and put to bed. For the next two hours they remain in bed, to sleep or at least rest. At 3:00 P.M. they are allowed to get up. The babies are cleaned, the older ones put on the pot again and given plenty of time to succeed. Another snack is distributed—whatever parents send along—and the children's play is supervised until 6:00.

Frau Heinimann, the plump, motherly director, has simple goals—give them love and teach them obedience. With over twenty children in a small play area, she and her assistant keep ahead of disturbances by imposing isolation on the recalcitrant child. The culprit who grabs a toy or pushes is warned. If he persists, he is placed sharply on a chair and told to stay there, is relegated to a play pen, or as a last resort, is sent back to bed. For those who become discontented or upset, a wafer, a pat, some rocking are tried—and there is always the *Schnuller,* [a rubber nipple on a plastic ring] the standard pacifier which hangs around the neck of most infants. It is a comman bedtime companion which, along with the child's blanket, is used to settle them for the nap.

The nursery is in operation from May 1 to November 1, the period of heavy farm work. The schedule has always been adjusted to agricultural working patterns and the needs of the extended family. If there are preschool children or babies in a farm family, grandparents are not ordinarily utilized as babysitters. They are of more economic value working in the fields or the vineyards. Some residents claim the nursery is peculiar to the hilly topography of the Engelskrone, that here the terraces are steep and irregular—dangerous for a mother who might bring a young child into the fields. Under any circumstances, the institution is functionally integrated into the agrarian character of the village life. Over 80 percent of the babies and young children enrolled come from farm families who must often arrange intricate systems of delivering their children to the nursery. Frau Dolbier has three children, two under three years, and one who is five-years-old. Each day she takes one of the younger babies on her bike to the nursery and has her five-year-old daughter push the other in a buggy. Then she lifts her daughter onto the bike and delivers her to a kindergarten.

Newcomers whose primary source of income is the factory make little use of the nursery. In the factory housing development a higher percentage of mothers do not work. If they do, their children are usually at least of kindergarten age. To deliver a three-month-old baby to public supervision is considered an act of desperation or parental irresponsibility. Factory parents make much greater use of kindergarten, to free the mother for work, and to expose the child to the kindergarten experience. But they usually do not commit their children to so long an enrollment as do native parents. The kindergarten program has a nativistic content about which some factory parents are reserved if not disdainful. Nevertheless, kindergarten constitutes an important institutional channel for creating personal contacts and affecting cultural interaction between factory and native families.

KINDERGARTEN

Rebhausen teachers claim they can invariably identify those first graders who have attended kindergarten. The children adjust more easily to school life. They work readily into the school routine, they play more cooperatively and skillfully with their classmates, and they are more familiar with traditional songs and poems. Distinct social and academic advantages appear to be immediately accessible to those who have experienced preschool training.

Most parents see that their children are enrolled for at least two years in one of the four kindergartens, all privately run by the two churches and geographically located to serve both residential patterns and religious interests. Approximately 225 children are registered in the four kindergartens, and the daily attendance averages close to 200, spread over an age range of from three to six years. With minor variations there is a basic routine common to all kindergartens:

8:00– 9:30	Free play.
9:30–11:00	Directed play starting with a story, usually from the Bible. The children may be asked to learn a Bible verse or song related to the story. If they have brought a snack with them, they are given a chance to eat it during this period.
11:00– 1:00	Lunch at home.
1:00– 1:30	Free play.
1:30– 3:00	Naptime, a period that may be foreshortened or even eliminated in the winter when the afternoon session is over at 4:30 or 5:00 P.M. There is always an afternoon nap during the summer when kindergarten is open until as late as 6:00 P.M.
3:00	Another snack. The kindergarten provides tea if the children have not brought something to drink.
3:30– 5:00	Free play and organized group activities.

The schedule reflects an adjustment to the occupational demands of parents, many of whom are farmers. For a mother the 8:00 A.M. beginning makes possible a sizeable morning's work in the fields. The 11:00 interruption presents no problem since she has to return home to prepare a hot meal for her husband. At about 1:00 P.M.—or later, if the weather is extremely hot—farm parents move back into the fields and are there, in the summer, until dusk. The afternoon closing time is adjusted to the season.

The implementation of the kindergarten program is a function not only of the church doctrine and control, the characteristics of the children, and the aspirations of parents, but also of the background of the teachers. Two of the regular kindergarten directors have widely divergent backgrounds—one young and trained in Berlin at a state teacher-training institute, the other elderly, a native of the area and trained by a special Evangelical church order of which she is a member. They both identify as a primary goal adjustment to the social group [*in die Gemeinschaft einordnen*]—learning to play with others and learning to accept the limits on individual behavior which group association requires. They are both concerned with isolates, the dangers of the condition, and techniques for handling it. Schwester Irene has directed a kindergarten in Rebhausen for over fifteen years, an experience which affords her a longitudinal perspective on Rebhausen children. She is interested in the changes in behavioral patterns the children are exhibiting. Ten years ago they were relatively quiet and subdued in their play, capable of absorbing themselves for relatively long periods with play objects and activities. Now, she claims, they are more lively and excitable and tend to move compulsively from one play situation to another rather rapidly. They are, as is so often mentioned by adults in Rebhausen, more nervous. She ascribes much of this development to television and the tempo of industrial life. She finds she can not conduct a Bible story hour on Monday or after a vacation. The children are too restless and need at least a day to work back into the routine. Frau Weber, from Berlin, finds the children quiet and phlegmatic in comparison with her earlier experience—easy to handle and more capable of playing cooperatively with each other. She finds it necessary to teach them better table manners, but she is pleased with the children. They are not as impudent as city children and when they tattle on a playmate it is not, she feels, so much an attempt to draw attention to themselves, as it is simply to report a rule is being broken.

Management of the kindergarten reflects concern for the development of appropriate social-civic behavior. Disciplinary techniques are firm but not overpowering. Children are isolated if their play is unsettling or disturbing. They are spanked if they lie or pick on other children or disturb little children who are sleeping. They are given a chance to perform minor duties on a volunteer basis—set the table and clean up the closets. They have to learn to play together; the play areas are small, the play equipment minimal, and the enrollment large. Spatial restrictions, which they tend to experience at home, are rendered not only through social relations but also through individual physical experiences. The sleeping room is crowded and during the nap period the children are, on even a warm day, equipped with blankets which most of them use.

The kindergartens observe the seasonal celebrations and traditions of Rebhausen and exploit parental interest in their children's progress. Christmas and Easter programs are organized and presented to parents. Orientation meetings are held for mothers; subjects such as "My child doesn't want to eat" are discussed. Mothers are taught songs or crafts the children are learning, so they can help at home.

The child who enters the first grade has experienced a relationship with adults in which obligations are clearly defined and infractions regularly and forcefully punished. The baby, in the crib or carriage, is the object of parental love and affection and of solicitous neighborly attention; preschool children, in all their innocent, wide-eyed, and amusing encounters with the social world they experience, are surrounded by an atmosphere of protective care. But these affective relationships do not appear to soften the pressures and social demands routinely imposed on young children by parents or by nursery and kindergarten personnel.

Because the social performance of the child carries a strong value judgment with respect to parental skill and success, the parental role in the incorporation process is characterized by a sense of urgency which manifest itself in early child-rearing practices. Those compressive forces, which in many societies are focused on a particular developmental stage in order to affect a dramatic change in role, are in Rebhausen evenly distributed along the growth continuum. The parent-child relationship is marked by a directing, pushing pressure on the part of parents, particularly the father. The extended family system appears to provide no muting influence; it distributes positive roles to relatives and consistently retains for parents the role of teacher and disciplinarian. The functional value of this relationship is clear. The kind of subordinate role the child learns in the home, he will experience in the school. The development of this role will be discussed in the next chapter which concerns the organization and content of school life.

3 / The school: organization, content, and procedure

ORGANIZATION

EDUCATION IN GERMANY is by tradition and authority the responsibility of the states. The organization of the schools, the employment and promotion of teachers, and the content of the curriculum are carefully supervised by the state Ministry of Education. Local communities must assume financial obligations for building and instructional materials, but they are aided by state subsidies. The Rebhausen elementary school is, therefore, a state school—one element in a system of public education which is intricately and thoroughly organized.

Although kindergarten is not compulsory, most children do attend. Eight years of elementary school is the traditional requirement.[1] The children enter the first grade at six or seven, remain in the elementary school for eight years, attend after graduation a part-time vocational school for three years during an apprenticeship, take their journeyman examination, and settle down to work. This pattern is typical for Rebhausen children and graduates of rural schools in general. The number of students in Rebhausen who leave the elementary school after four or five years to enter a *Gymnasium* has increased since the factory was built. But the number is small (10 out of 95 in 1965). Prior to 1964 it had been typical for no more than two or three students to make the transfer.

Intermediate schools provide entrees into commercial and business vocations, *Gymnasien* into universities and the professions. The nearest intermediate schools and *Gymnasien* are located in Waldstadt; those few students who choose to attend these schools and who are admitted to them must commute each day. Most of the vocational schools in the vicinity are also in Waldstadt. Elementary school graduates customarily commute once or twice a week.

The teachers are employees of the state. Their mandate originates in the state constitution which asserts that:

> The education of youth is to be oriented toward a reverence of God, the spirit of Christian charity, the love of nation and home, moral and political responsibility, vocational and social integrity, and a free democratic commitment. . . .

The state Ministry of Education is charged with organizing, directing, and evaluating the implementation of this mandate. Consequently, the curriculum plan and the

---

[1] A ninth year has recently been added and must be implemented by 1970.

course content is outlined in careful detail in curriculum publications and distributed to each school to be implemented.

The basic curriculum publication for elementary schools gives attention not only to the instructional program of the school but also to the tone and tenor of school life itself. The elementary school is charged with developing the human and social powers of the pupils and through this development affecting and evolving a school life in which each student is a responsible participant. The publication emphasizes that the decisive factor in the instructional and educational program of the school is the personality of the teacher.

The state directives do not preclude the possibility that individual schools will evolve procedures and arrangements peculiar to the characteristics of the community and to the professional interests of the teachers. In this respect, the directive to the rural school is explicit. In practice, however, these general directives and goals are supplemented by a continuous flow of administrative directives from the state to local authorities, covering almost every conceivable exigency. (This relationship will be examined in detail in a subsequent chapter.) Consequently, the domain of maneuverability for a local school is highly restricted. The class schedule, requirements for which originate at the state level, is the primary administrative arrangement through which the state structures education at the community level.

The first encounter with a class schedule in a German school is a bewildering experience. A cursory examination provokes the uneasy feeling that the schedule is a kind of I.Q. test, to measure a pupil's capacity to adjust to a totally new way of life, and that success requires a flair for bureaucratic nuances. In the first weeks of a school year, pupils have to develop a certain hyper-consciousness of each succeeding day's hourly plan, and a few parents like to post a copy of the schedule by their bedside. The schedule reflects a curriculum plan that encompasses a variety of subject-matter areas and that requires a compartmentalized treatment of these subjects over a period of years. Inherent in the schedule is the assumption that education is a cumulative process which can maintain its integrity and utility only through a carefully structured arrangement of reinforcement.

The first grader is not subjected to the total sweep of the curriculum. His school week totals approximately 18 hours (as compared with 28–31 hours for upper classes), and the curriculum he experiences is more generalized.

1. Unified instruction: 16 hours
    a. German: 8 hours
    b. Community life: 4 hours
    c. Arithmetic: 3 hours
    d. Physical education: 1 hour
2. Home economics: 1 hour (girls only)

Beginning with the third grade, courses are specifically delineated, and during the last four years of school, the schedule establishes the following hourly distribution over a week.

1. Religion: 3 hours
2. Geography: 2 hours

3. History: 2 hours
4. Civics: 1 hour
5. German: 6 hours
6. Arithmetic: 4 hours
7. Geometry: 1 hour
8. Natural science: 2 hours
9. General science: 2 hours
10. Drawing: 1 hour
11. Music: 2 hours
12. Physical education: 2 hours
13. Shop-home economics: 2 hours

The distribution is spread over a school week of six days and a school day of eight hours, only five of which are generally scheduled for any grade. If a student is scheduled for classes in the afternoon (not more than twice a week), morning classes do not begin until the third or fourth period. No afternoon classes are scheduled on Saturday. There is a five-minute recess between each fifty-minute period and a fifteen-minute mid-morning recess between the second and third period. One hour is provided at noon. More time is actually available for this meal; with afternoon classes a student will have a free period before or after the lunch hour.

The school day was once simply arranged. The four upper grades were scheduled for the morning, and free in the afternoon to help with the farm chores. The four lower grades had classes in the afternoon. This schedule was a common experience of most Rebhausen adults and a constant reminder that the school existed to serve the agricultural interests and needs of the community. The present schedule, infinitely more complicated, is just as stark a reminder that the school no longer has one dominant economic activity to serve and one type of pupil to educate. Afternoon classes remain especially repugnant to farmers, many of whom associate such scheduling complications with the presence and influence of the factory rather than simply with the attendant population growth and changing times. They feel it ignores the farmer and placates the factory personnel.

Teachers accept afternoon classes as necessary but not desirable, and they have the normal interest in the kind of specific class arrangement which will be appropriate to their professional interests. Before the opening of school, they engage in negotiations with each other. Based on the knowledge they have of particular interests among their colleagues, they maneuver to avoid the subjects they do not like and to have their favorite subjects located at the most advantageous part of the day. The process requires a victim. Herr Greiner, the assistant principal and senior member of the faculty with over twenty-five years of service in Rebhausen, usually assumes the responsibility of drawing up a schedule. Each year during spring vacation he takes time to sketch out a schedule—never, apparently, with any overwhelming degree of success.

Schedule-making is routine but never smooth. Before the end of the school year, class assignments are made by the principal, with due regard for the personal attachments of teachers to classes they are already teaching. Herr Greiner devotes a good part of his vacation to making out the schedule, and he presents it to the faculty on the first day of school. There are groans and protests, and when the meeting ends, further negotiating and maneuvering are initiated. Herr Doering, who up to this point has managed to avoid the process, is appealed to for help and forced to assume an intervening role. The confusion continues for the better part of a week, during which time the teachers make daily adjustments and have the students write notes to themselves to keep track of the changes. By the end of the week the schedule is settled. Some compromises are usually affected, but most such efforts are

The end of a school day—the old building.

defeated by the unbending bureaucratic tyranny which curriculum requirements impose on the schedule-making process.

CLASSROOM PROCEDURE

First grade. The rapid population growth of the village is reflected in class sizes; in each of the past three years the entering class has been large enough to require two sections. The two first grade teachers for the present school year are Fraulein Wollner, a young, pleasant, unmarried girl who is intensely occupied with her teaching responsibilities, and Frau Reuter, wife of the fifth grade teacher, an attractive woman in her late thirties who is often absent from the classroom due to illness. Fraulein Wollner is particularly conscious of classroom procedure. As a beginning teacher her status is probationary; she must have another year of teaching experience, pass a written and oral examination, and stand an inspection of her teaching performance before she can be classified in a permanent civil service status. Frau Reuter is an experienced teacher who prefers a limited teaching load and the part-time classification that goes with it.

Reading is naturally of primary importance in the first grade. The basic reading method centers on the complete word rather than single letters, an innovation of recent years. Older Rebhausen generations remember the intricate drawing exercises they had to perform and the esoteric processes that were invented to describe how letters are put together. In recent years, when the size of the school made two sections necessary, the school began experimenting with the word system. The choice of method was more a matter of training and personal preference on the part of individual teachers, but an effort was made to ascertain the utility of the two methods. The experiment was short-lived; parents objected to the lack of unity.

After five months of school, the class is reading short passages which give them practice with different letters in the alphabet. The following one is typical.

> Hans has a wheel. The wheel is his carrousel. Come, children, come! Once around costs only a mark. There come Lotte and Susi, Kurt and Berta, Hans and Karl. There comes the cat Fifi.

They talk about the story first, about what the children are doing in the picture. Then they read, a few alone, then together by aisles, finally the entire class. Word cards are regularly used.

The teaching of German is divided into five primary categories: oral expression, reading, written expression, grammar, and handwriting, all areas to which first graders are introduced. A particularly distinctive device for teaching correct grammar and spelling is dictation. The state course of instruction requires that by the end of the fourth year children should, within the range of their vocabulary, be able to write dictation selections without making many errors. At this point in the year Fraulein Wollner is giving dictation to first graders in the form of short sentences: the lady comes, the ship arrives, the fish want water. The children write the sentences in their dictation notebook, and when they finish, she collects the notebooks and writes the sentences on the blackboard.

After five months of school, homework has developed into something more demanding than the assignments in the early weeks. A typical assignment is: four sentences using the word "come," four sentences using the word "rush," two sets of arithmetic exercises, and pictures to color. The theme of the pictures, which they have drawn in class, is "I help mother."

Although Fraulein Wollner is a beginning teacher, she displays no uncertainties about her responsibilities as a disciplinarian and is particularly sensitive to unacceptable behavior that occurs when she is at the blackboard with her back turned. On one occasion, when she was writing a dictation, she turned around suddenly to find a boy in the back waving his hands at her. She stalked to the back, cuffed him soundly, and returned to finish her writing. After the class we discussed methods of discipline. She observed that teachers are not supposed to use physical punishment, at least in the first grade, but she finds she has to—the children listen better when they know they might be punished in this manner.

Fraulein Wollner makes productive use of class disapproval to affect changes in the performance of children. When, for example, a pupil is called to the front to recite and has nothing to say, she sends him back to his seat and often starts the class singing the following:

Alle Leut, alle Leut stehen früh auf.	[All the people get up early.
Lang-schläfer, auf-gewacht!	Sleepy-head, wake up!
Draussen die Sonne lacht!	Outside the sun beams!
Alle Leut, alle Leut stehen früh auf.	All the people get up early.]

At the end of the song the whole class gleefully turns toward the pupil and points at him. Fraulein Wollner thinks it helps them to be more attentive.

The children learn that the system of behavior control is not implemented by the teacher alone but by students as well, through both officially and unofficially sanctioned uses of authority. The traffic patrol, composed of seventh and eighth graders, not only supervises school pedestrian traffic when there are movements to and from the building, but is also charged with reporting to the classrooms at the end of recess and supervising behavior until the teachers return. We came back after one recess to find the names of three boys on the blackboard. Fraulein Wollner called the boys to the front and demanded an explanation. Their responses were hesitant, but other members of the class chimed in with accounts of their behavior. She grabbed each one firmly by the hair, shook him, and told him to behave.

Since the state course of instruction is very detailed, the class routine and progress in both sections of the first grade are similar. Frau Reuter has special interests, however, and works extensively with the children in the field of music, using rhythm instruments. She has a careful routine especially developed for physical education classes: body exercises, marching around the hall, jumping rope, climbing a ladder, a game of elimination using a volley ball. The order she wants to impose on this routine requires constant attention and rearrangement; the children participate with an intense excitement and abandon that is not easily restrained. Any sudden change in the fortunes of individuals participating in the games is punctuated with loud screams. In the marching column, the boys in particular exploit opportunities to push and shove and fall down.

The behavior of the children in the physical education periods seems to be characterized by a drive for release from the restraints of the classroom. This is also true of behavior during recess. Classrooms are emptied and the children sent outside. Their play is active and unorganized. The girls play simple games or stand around talking. The boys run, often wildly and compulsively; they chase each other, push and wrestle. The playground is the area between the school building and the *Turnhalle,* a space approximately thirty by fifteen yards. There are, with 400 children in various states of energetic play, predictable accidents: skinned knees and bumps, once in a while a broken bone. To cut down on the possibility of serious injury, Herr Doering ruled out running. The teacher with playground duty enforced the rule, but only with diligence and constant haranguing of the students. The students responded by developing a fast walk. In about two weeks the faculty, by unwritten consent, gave up on the effort, and running is as prevalent as ever.

Second grade.   Frau Borner is a Rebhausen native whose husband, an army officer, was once principal of the school. She is a soft-spoken person with a style of teaching that is methodical and relatively gentle. Multiplication drills are a good example. The second grade is working on 7's, 8's and 9's. Students are called on; if one is slow in answering, she sometimes observes, *"Er hat nicht ausgeschlafen,"* [He didn't get enough sleep.] If no answer is forthcoming, the pupil stands by his desk until the right answer is given. This is routine, but sometimes she has to halt them [*"Bleib stehen"*] when they start to sit down. It is a mild form of punishment for unpreparedness or inadequacy. A pupil whose ignorance is exposed can not quickly retire and ignore the failure. He has to remain attentive until he is rescued by a classmate, a process that might take five minutes. Sometimes a pupil remains standing after the right answer is given, until the teacher tells him to sit down; sometimes he decides himself he can retreat and simply eases back into his seat.

There is much unison work on the multiplication tables, rendered with a rhythm that is almost hypnotic in its effect. Frau Borner also finds it useful to make a game of learning the tables. Slips of paper with simple problems are handed out to half the class, and the answers to the other half. The pupils appear to be totally involved in the game. When a problem is read and the answer not immediately given, the rest of the class—at least those who know—react immediately. They shake their hands excitedly, snap their fingers, turn and jump in their seats. The reaction is just as energetic if a pupil, demonstrating a problem at the board, makes a mistake. They are eager to get credit for being able to make the correction.

Heimatkunde [community life] in the second grade exploits the needs and experiences of children growing up in an agricultural, rural environment. The topics covered during the year include the following:

1. Now we are second graders; school rules and acceptable behavior.
2. Traffic instruction: crossing streets, use of bikes.
3. Spring comes: flowers and animals wake up.
4. Our birds.
5. Hay harvest: the work of the farmer.
6. The cherry tree and its guests.
7. On the farm.
8. A storm: how it develops, what we see, how we react.
9. Flowers in the fields.
10. The grain harvest.
11. A wine harvest.
12. Protection of animals
13. People who serve us: doctors and nurses.
14. Health is the best protection.
15. People prepare for winter.
16. The time of Christmas.
17. The work of the people in the community.
18. The important buildings in the community.

19. At the gas station.
20. At the post office
21. At the railroad station
22. Easter: the easter rabbit comes

The discussion of good health is lively. Frau Borner asks how they would treat an open wound. She cautions them against the use of water; it might be contaminated. One boy proposes *Schnaps* which is not considered a bad idea. They discuss good eating habits; she tells them to avoid food and drinks that are too hot or too cold because extreme temperatures are bad for the stomach. They talk about the care of teeth; she asks how many of them brushed their teeth that morning. The response is three out of twenty, and she tells them she will ask them again the next morning. The response then is better, ten out of twenty.

The second grader's experiences are not unlike those of the first grader in the development of intra-class disciplinary pressures. Frau Borner structures relationships to encourage pupil participation in the process of discipline, and in the more informal moments of interaction with pupils, she does not discourage the initiative they assert in this area. She uses student monitors for duty when she is in the classroom as well as when she is absent. It is her custom while writing material at the blackboard to have a monitor stand beside her and face the class—to report those who misbehave. From the custom, the children themselves learn both that it is acceptable to report misbehavior and what constitutes publicly unacceptable behavior. The complaints that are voiced include the following: He's looking at my work. she's bothering me by talking, she's leaning back too far and pushing my books, he pulled one of the paper chickens down from the wall. They learn too that the process of discipline is going on in other classes. If a teacher wants to assign a student to extra work after school [*Arrest*] or simply wants to remove him from the class— and the teacher does not want to stay after school himself—he generally finds a class which is meeting in the afternoon and arranges for the pupil to sit in it while doing the work. Since Frau Borner's class usually meets in the afternoon, older students are sometimes working in the back.

Third grade.   On the Rebhausen faculty are six men and six women. Grade assignments are generally made with the women in the lower grades and the men in the upper grades. Since it is also traditional that teachers stay with a class two, three, or even four years (from the first through the third grades, or the sixth through the eighth), the distribution of teachers by sex among the grades varies. During my year in Rebhausen only one male teacher had a class as low as the third grade. Herr Könecke is in his early forties and had for many years been a businessman. Because of a labor shortage and other problems encountered in running his grocery, he decided to enter teaching and is now in his second year of probation.

Herr Könecke is a short, stocky individual with craggy features, friendly and loquacious among his colleagues, brusque and demanding with his pupils. The lesson he conducts in *Heimatkunde* [local history] affords the pupils an introduction to the responsibilities of local governing officials, especially the mayor, and also illustrates the thoroughness with which pupils are led to a mastery of the spoken and written language. Herr Könecke solicits from the class ideas about who the officials are and what they do. As the discussion develops, he weaves their responses into a paragraph on the blackboard.

> The chief official at the Rathaus is the mayor. He concerns himself with the welfare of the village. He orders the construction and repair of streets, water and sewer lines, and public buildings such as the school. He draws up contracts with construction firms. The mayor is aided in his work by his staff. Some of them type letters which he dictates.

When he completes the paragraph, he has them copy it in their notebook—a procedure common to all the classes. Much of the knowledge which the pupils accumulate and for which they are responsible is acquired in this manner.

The school budget allows a reasonable amount for the purchase of instructional materials, but minimal from the standpoint of affecting opportunities for more versatility in instructional techniques. The purchase of materials is a local responsibility, so Herr Doering and the faculty must ask the mayor and the *Gemeinderat* for financial help. The personal aspects of this kind of transaction are complicated. At the same time, state law makes it mandatory for schools to provide free textbooks —if individual parents so petition. This, too, is a complicated social and interpersonal process. It is traditional for parents to purchase the materials. Teachers work to maintain the tradition by requiring the minimal number of textbooks, partly in the hopes that the village will then have more money available for school purchases they consider more important. But this policy has behind it a pedagogical as well as an economic rationale. The widespread use of notebooks to copy dictation and material placed on the blackboard increases the control the teacher exercises over the learning content and the distribution of time needed to establish that content.

Herr Könecke, although a new teacher, asserts an aggressive, commanding, and sometimes intimidating authority in the classroom. When he moves down the aisles, inspecting students' work as they do arithmetic exercises, his reaction to erros or sloppy work is brusque and pointed: he pulls hair, twists ears, slaps the back of the head, or often exclaims in dismay, *"Mensch, Mensch!"* [man, man!"] This kind of treatment is reserved for boys, some of whom attempt to adjust to it by ducking or crouching down in their seats. When he hands back tests, he announces the score of each student (a common practice in the school) and has the student come up to the front to get his paper. The presentation is accompanied by some appropriate remark, sometimes jesting and friendly, often rough and sarcastic. For the poorer student there is no anonymity or secrecy behind which he can hide. Since Herr Könecke has the poorer students assigned to rows on the far side of the room, so that he can "work with them better," their general performance is already well publicized.

But this kind of teaching presence does not seem to affect the overt interest such pupils exhibit in classroom procedures. Their desire to recite, or to participate in other activities, is characterized by an eagerness which seems to indicate a normal adjustment to and acceptance of the demands laid upon them. The musical and art activities Herr Könecke organizes are administered in the same commanding tone, but they provide a release from the academic routine, which pleases the children immensely. Furthermore, such activities have inherent appeal for childern whose experience with play materials is limited. The artwork he brings in—for example, a Christmas design that they use in making decorations—represents not only his careful, skillful work but also the chance for the pupils to explore a medium that has immediate appeal.

State law requires that, beginning with the third grade, a dictation is given every two weeks and a short essay assigned every three weeks. The topics are varied and afford an enlightening source of information about the children's experiences and feelings in a variety of life activities. *"Eine Ohrfeige"* is a traditional theme for third graders. An *Ohrfeige* is, according to the standard translation, a box on the ear. From my observations and the children's descriptions it tends, however, to be a sharp slap on the face and apparently a typical, almost automatic reaction of parents to unacceptable behavior. The essays the children wrote are really paragraphs, concise and often colorfully expressed. They know all about *Ohrfeigen,* and the ones described sound as if they were the last—because the children are sure they have learned an important lesson.

They receive *Ohrfeigen* for sloppy homework.

Dieter Laufenberger

I was doing my homework, then Mother said I should make it pretty. After that I finished. Then my mother came and looked at the notebook again. I got an *Ohrfeige*. I went to the table and started to improve the homework. Then a car went by and I went to the window and forgot all about my homework. Then I got another *Ohrfeige*.

They get *Ohrfeigen* for quarreling.

Gunter Schupp

Once when I came home my sister was already there. I thought, however, as I stood in the yard, that she wasn't there. Then I saw her and we started to quarrel. Then my father came home. He saw us quarreling and, bang, I got one behind the ear. I said, "It wasn't my fault; it was my sister's." Hardly had I said that when, bang, I got another one. By the second *Ohrfeige* I saw stars. But that finished the quarreling. On such days there's usually an *Ohrfeige*.

They get *Ohrfeigen* for making flimsy excuses when they break a dish or try to conceal a misdemeanor.

Hans Brümmel

An *Ohrfeige* usually comes quickly and unexpectedly. There was one that really hurt. I had to buy some meat but on the way lost the money. I looked for it in despair. A friend came and helped me look. All of a sudden he said, "The butcher will give you meat without money." I did it and, in spite of having a bad conscience, I said nothing at home. When my parents got the bill, there was a storm and my mother pulled back her hand. That was the *Ohrfeige* that I'll never forget as long as I live.

They get *Ohrfeigen* from older brothers and sisters when they do not obey.

Jutta Kiefer

When I came home one day from school, no one was there, only my sister. She said to me, "Wash the dishes and clean the kitchen; I'm going out." Then I said, "I don't have any time. Wash them yourself. I could also go out." Boom, she gave me a real *Ohrfeige*. The next time I washed the dishes and obeyed my sister.

They get them from strangers.

Gisela Metzger

It was a beautiful day. I went out into the street to play ball with my friends. For awhile we had a good time. Then an auto came by and we ran to get out of the way. The ball was still bouncing. And what happened? The ball bounced hard against the window of the car. We couldn't run away. The driver stopped and climbed angrily out. He yelled at us, and, whack, each of us received a well-earned *Ohrfeige*. From that I learned the lesson never again to play ball in the street.

Sometimes they enjoy the chance to give an *Ohrfeige*.

Helga Buchheit

When my brother and I were home alone one day I had to cook the noon meal. There was apple sauce and noodles. I noticed that there wasn't any more sugar. I told Fritz he should go to the store and get two pounds of sugar. But he didn't want to go. Then I said, "You know what mother said. You must obey me, because I am in the third grade and you're only in the second. Are you going or aren't you? He answered, "No!" Then I gave him an *Ohrfeige* so hard that he almost fell down. After that he obeyed me.

They receive *Ohrfeigen* for getting their clothes dirty, for breaking windows, for not quieting down at night after they have gone to bed, for talking back, for not eating properly or fast enough. They are accustomed to *Ohrfeigen,* so what they experience at school, of physical punishment, is no deviation from what they experience at home.

The third graders wrote other themes during the year, for example, on the subject, "What makes me happy." Most of them wrote of the end of winter and the pleasures of warm weather. They convey a lyrical joy in nature's bounty.

Gunter Schupp

When the winter hangs on and the ice and snow don't melt I'm unhappy. When however spring comes and the first snow drops, cowslips, and violets bloom, I'll be happy that finally winter is at an end, and when we can go swimming and learn to swim. In vacation I can take a hike with my comrades, because I like very much to hike.

Angelika Buch

After a long cold winter spring finally comes again. I am happy when buds first appear on trees. Yesterday I found two little violets as I was walking around the house. How wonderful it will be when summer comes when we can swim again and when the flowers bloom. I also enjoy the warm summer air. When the birds sing so happily, I want above all to sing with them. All that makes me happy and joyful.

Some of the children understandably find their greatest joy in vacation, the end of school.

Playing among the terraces.

Susanne Kasbohm

When I think about it, that vacation will soon come then I am really happy. Because then I can go where I want to. I don't have to do any more homework because vacation is vacation. Although I like to go to school, vacations are much better. Soon it will be vacation and then I'll be happier than I ever was before. Vacations are always the best in the world.

For a few pupils, there are dreams of joyous moments characterized by humor and pathos.

Horst Eschenauer

It makes me happy when the sun shines and it is wonderfully dry out. Then it's nice to go out. It would make me happy if I were permitted to drive a motor-boat all day long, and didn't get a thrashing from my father. It would make me happy if I could thrash my father once the way he does me.

Dorothea Orlemann

Most of all I'd like to have a good friend. Because no one likes me. All the others stay together and keep secrets from me. Often they look at me suspiciously, and when I come near them they quickly say to each other, "Be quiet, Dorothea is coming." Then they act as if nothing were wrong. When they buy something for the teacher, they want me to give some money too, but as soon as they have my money they get rid of me. They're always unjust. I can't ever be happy because I'm always thinking of their injustice to me. So it's my deepest wish to have a friend.

They wrote a theme on a time when they had been really scared. They described mysterious noises in the cellar, barking dogs after dark, strangers in cars who suddenly stopped to ask questions or who tried to get them to get into the car, the prospect of a severe spanking for some misdemeanor, and solitary walks in the village forest. Most frequently described was an evening at home, alone.

Gilbert Koll

One time my parents went out for an evening. After they left I went right to bed. I stayed awake for a couple of hours. Suddenly I heard something tapping. It came nearer and nearer and finally someone rattled the door knob. I was really frightened. Then this person unlocked the door. I hid under the bed and thought a gangster was coming in. Then he came in. He turned on the light, looked in all the rooms and when he came to my room I saw that it was my brother. Then he asked me, "What are you doing there?" I answered him, "What am I doing here? I'm not doing anything." And my fear was gone.

Adelhaid Kellner

One morning my mother said to me, "This evening we want to go out a little." That made me happy. Then she said, "If someone knocks, don't open the door." When mommy and daddy left I was happy. But all of a sudden there was a knock at the door and I was really frightened. The noise went on and I began to cry. I was really happy when my parents came home. My mother asked if anything had happened and I told her. "But you didn't open the door," she said. "Oh, no," I told her, "but I was really frightened." Now my parents don't go out evenings.

They wrote themes on how they could do something nice for their mother especially on Mother's Day.

Petra Methfessel

I get up early in the morning, get dressed and go into the kitchen. I get a white table cloth and set the table. I get the cake and put it on the table. Then I make coffee. I fill up a pot with water and put it on the stove to heat. Then I get the electric coffee grinder from the cabinet and grind coffee. When the coffee is ground I get the coffee pot and the filter. Then I put the coffee on the table and get the present for Mother's day. Then I wake my mother. When she sees the present she is very happy. Then I recite the poem and give her a kiss.

They wrote of other festive occasions, of Christmas and Easter.

Wolfgang Epp

There's one time of year that's really nice. That's the time around Advent and before Christmas. Advent means that the Holy One comes. Then it all smells of bread, and cake, and chocolate. We can see our mother bringing big packages home from the stores and we can see her hide them somewhere in the house. We can hear mommy and daddy talking with each other. We can hear "You stay in the kitchen," and she shuts the door. Then we hear them talk some more, but we can't understand them. But soon it'll be Christmas. We've already waited a long time for it.

Gerhard Schlatterer

In the night before Easter I could hardly sleep I was so excited. My mother had told me I'd faint when I saw the present from grandmother. Sure enough when my grandmother came she brought me a bike. I was too surprised to say anything. It was a few weeks before I could really believe it belonged to me. Then I went with grandmother to the mountains.

These examples of student writing and those that follow are in style and content representative of the class from which they come and reflect the emphasis on writing characteristic of all grades.

Fourth grade. There is a noticeable change between the third and fourth grades in the quantity of work demanded. The change is to be explained not in terms of teachers but in terms of the organization of the state-wide system of education. Transfer from the elementary school to a *Gymnasium,* leading to university study, takes place either in the fourth or fifth grades, usually at the end of the fourth. The selection process begins in late November with a state testing program in German (essay and dictation) and arithmetic. All fourth and fifth graders take the exams, administered on five different days over a period of a month. It is the intent of the Ministry of Education that the testing program be integrated into the regular classroom program and that no special announcements, arrangements (other than on the days of the tests) or preparations be made. Practically speaking, a fourth or fifth grade teacher is going to be concerned that the class is adequately prepared and that at least those few pupils whose parents want them to transfer to a *Gymnasium* and who possess the basic qualifications will perform acceptably. Consequently, Frau Schenke, the fourth grade teacher, was concentrating, in October and November, on essay writing, dictation, and arithmetic. Dictations were being given every week, instead of the required every two weeks. At this point they have become more detailed and precise in their content. For example:

On both sides of the Rhine River are fertile plains and quaint, picturesque villages. Grain of all kinds, tobacco and potatoes are planted in great quantities and bring the farmers ample reward for the year's work. Forests of fruit trees surround the villages and provide us tasty apples and juicy peaches. Further inland terraces are planted with grapevines. From them we get sweet-tasting grapes and fine wine. Everywhere in the country there is an air of prosperity, and farmers hope that a sudden and fierce storm will not destroy the crops.

In arithmetic work has progressed to practice on story problems. A typical homework assignment consists of two problems:

1. At a sports event seats cost 1.50 DM, standing-room 1 DM, and a student ticket 0.50 DM. 294 seats were sold and 2782 standing-room tickets. The total amount taken in was 4035 DM. How many student tickets were sold?
2. A truck is carrying 1800 liters of oil in barrels each of which holds 150 liters and costs 72 DM. The cost of transportation is 8 DM. What is the total cost of the load?

Homework assignments are usually due the next day. The papers are graded and returned in the usual public ceremony. Grades range from one to six. Frau Schenke hands back the papers, reads the range of grades, and then has the students stand up, according to the grades they receive, starting with the poorest mark. It is a break in the routine. The pupils watch with interest as the "6s" stand up. There is a ripple of excitement when it is obvious that someone has done more poorly than expected. The same is true of the "1s,"; there are audible expressions of admiration when an average pupil breaks through to the top.

The similarity of some of the errors one day indicated to Frau Schenke the likelihood of copying, especially since these particular papers had been written by pupils sitting next to each other. She accused them of copying. They mumbled an excuse but she pressed them until they lapsed into silence. No action was taken, a fact which often characterizes disciplinary procedure. The behavioral norms and rules imposed on the class are numerous. A logical and complete administration of each violation, even when it is serious, would demand a great deal of the teacher's time. Consequently, punishment is often limited to public exposure and denunciation. When, for example, Frau Schenke has long lines of children at her desk waiting to have their work graded, she stations a pupil at the blackboard to write down the names of those who are disorderly. In the days I observed the class, the names accumulated in one period numbered as high as 10, some with *x*'s indicating multiple violations. At the end of the period the monitor usually erases the names after Frau Schenke has glanced at them. If the *x*'s are too frequent, she asks the class what happened. She chooses, she says, pupils as monitors who are *anständig* [well-behaved]. If incidents of disorderliness are too severe, she whips the boys across the fingers with a stick or sends them to a nearby classroom to write an extra assignment.

The essays the fourth graders wrote give evidence of more attention to detail; they are longer and more expressive. Accounts of *Ohrfeigen* include more examples of ones they have given rather than received—and are at times rather philosophical.

Joachim Kaiser

One time I went walking. First I went down a street a little while and than I came to a path through a field. I followed it for a long time until I came to a spring. It was a hot day and the sun burned. I was very thirsty and drank from the brook. Everything was quiet; you couldn't hear a thing. Suddenly I saw a little boy. He picked up a stone and threw it at me. That hurt but the pain didn't last long. I chased him and gave him a slap in the face. He cried and went home. I walked on because I wanted to go into the forest. When I got to the forest, I sat down and ate something. Then I went home. When I got there may parents asked me if it had been nice. I answered yes and told them the story.

Anita Reichhardt

One day after school we started home. On the way I met a classmate. He asked me where I had been so long. I told him, "That's none of your business." I was angry and slapped him. On the next day his mother came to our house and told my mother all about it. My mother called me. I didn't pay any attention. After a while she came to get me. I ran outside. She came after me and the woman began to tell it again. I got a real good slap from my mother. The woman went home. Later my mother asked me, "Why do you act that way?" I didn't answer. So it goes in life. The proverb is, "Whoever digs a grave for someone else, falls in himself."

Bertold Feuchter

Last week, Sunday night, we didn't have anything to do. I went into the children's room and looked in the cabinet to see if I could find a good game to play. I saw the *Dame-Mühle* game. I came back a few minutes later into the living room and said to my father, "Papa, shall we play *Dame?*" He didn't say no and we played but I always lost. Then my mother said, "You're a loser." I got angry and said, "You always lose too." I got a slap in the face. Then I thought, "That I'll never forget," but I played again.

Frau Schenke assigned them topics to remind them to take better care of their possessions. They wrote one on an incident in class.

Ingrid Bergau

Our teacher said today to Anita, "Bring me your briefcase." Then Frau Schenke told her to sit down in front. The teacher took the satchel and looked in. She shook all the junk out. I got the wastebasket. Then she asked us, "What have I just done?" We answered the question. Then we went to work. The teacher and I threw old paper, two or three old notebooks, and an old empty drawing pad into the wastebasket. Then Anita lay down on the bench and began to cry. Gustav said, "You don't need to cry. It happened to me too." We laughed loud. When we had thrown away the paper we piled the notebooks and papers on top of each other and put them in the satchel. The books and small notebooks we stood straight up, the big notebooks we put in crossways. Then we closed the satchel and said to her, "Hopefully it'll look better tomorrow."

She had them write about funny tricks they had played.

Heinz Gruber

Once when my uncle was visiting us my brother and I played a trick on him. In the evening there was a good program on television. My uncle turned on the set and asked me if I would get him a box of cigars. My brother was outside. I went out and he asked me who I had to get the cigars for. I said, "for Uncle Willy." Then I got the cigars. My brother said, "Give me a cigar." He took one and went to his friend Manfred who had a horse. He told him his plan. Manfred got some scissors and cut a hair off the horse. Then he took a needle and pulled the horsehair through the cigar. He gave it to me and I gave it to my uncle. He lit the cigar and puffed on it. All of a sudden he almost fainted. The horsehair stank and smoked. He threw the cigar in the stove. Since then he gets his cigars himself.

The academic program pupils follow at the end of the fourth grade is an overpowering determinant of subsequent vocational choices. Those who leave the elementary school and enter a *Gymnasium* are oriented toward university training and the professions. Those who remain (a very large majority) in the elementary school are committed to farming, to vocations such as masonry and carpentry, to commercial pursuits such as bookeeping, or to teaching at the kindergarten or elementary school level. It is possible, but extremely difficult to move during the last four years in the elementary school into the university track. Few do. But the factory, the presence of factory personnel children in the classrooms, the rising standard of living, and full employment are factors working to create new vocational aspirations among the parents and children.

Since the state provides vocational counseling in the last years of the elementary school and since the fourth grade is a crucial point in the whole process, I was interested in finding out what thought children of this age had already given to vocational choices. Frau Schenke assigned an essay, "What I'd like to be some day." The paragraphs are written as letters to a relative or godparent.

Joachim Kaiser

Dear Uncle Fritz! Now I want to write you. I've wanted to write you for a long time, I want to ask you what I should learn to be. You know I don't like to work in the fields. I'd rather do hand work. My father doesn't want that because I am his only son. I'd like the work of an electrician. I'd have to learn a lot but it would be interesting. I thought that you, dear Uncle Fritz, could talk with my father sometime. You can do that better than I can. I'm not through with school yet. It'll be a few years until I finish school. In the meantime things can change. The work of an electrician would really please me.

Fritz Junker

What I want to be, I don't know exactly. I'd like to be a truck driver, but my parents always say they wouldn't let me. Because it's very dangerous nowadays with so many cars on the road. If a person wants to be a truck driver, he needs a lot of money to buy a truck. But when one is a truck driver you get to travel all around. A truck driver isn't permitted to drink alcohol. That's hard for me to take because I like to drink wine. I'm very young, so everything can change before I am through with school.

Anita Reichhardt

I have decided when I finish school that I want to be a saleswoman, I like that vocation the best. I often stand and watch to see how saleswomen have to work. Best of all I'd like to learn such a vocation in a big department store in Wald-stadt. In a department store there are many beautiful things to sell, and I'd like that. I'd also like it to be able to ride the train each morning and evening. In a department store you have to wait on many people. As a saleswoman I'd always have to be nicely dressed and always have to be nice to the people who want to buy something.

The results are in some ways typical of the age level—that is, uncertain, romantic, idealized. But they add material on parent-child interaction with respect to vocational choices and indicate a movement toward vocational aspirations not typical of Rebhausen in previous years.

Fifth grade.   Fifth graders were asked to write a short essay on an interesting job. The range of vocations selected and described, for all the visionary qualities some of the choices had, exceed markedly the kinds of vocations they can observe directly in Rebhausen and reflect a strain toward independence from the tradition of choosing a parental vocation. However the question of vocational choice might be resolved some day, some boys are already experiencing sizeable pressures to develop an interest in the paternal vocation. At the end of the class session when the essays were written and had been handed in, one boy asked if he could have his paper back to erase one of the vocations he had listed as not being interested in. It was his father's vocation and the boy was scared his father would see the list. Another boy describes the struggle he lost.

Bernhand Tesch

My vocation is a problem because I would like to become an auto mechanic, but my father has a big carpentry business. He says, "You just want to run around with cars. You must become a carpenter. We need men to help us." My mother nodded in agreement. To be honest, I didn't want to just run around. I really like the job of a mechanic. It doesn't suit me to be a carpenter. But all the people say it would be better if I became one. So I have decided to become a carpenter. After I had made quite a few small things I found out that it was the best.

The boys chose mechanics (6), farmer (4), farmer and truck driver (4), mason (3), police (3), sailor (2), actor, goldsmith, pilot, translator, fireman, machinist, painter, butcher, cook, and electrician. No boy picked farming whose father was not himself a farmer. No boy was content to remain at the level of training of his father if the latter were classified as unskilled labor. Deviations from paternal vocations were more likely with nonagricultural occupations.

The girls' choice of vocational interests is also suggestive of a deviation from the typical pattern. It has been traditional for girls to attend a two year school in home economics after finishing the elementary school. Not one of them listed that course of action as an interesting vocation. Their selections are in general practical and attainable: registered nurse (7), saleswoman (5), kindergarten teacher (3), hairdresser (2), teacher (2), stewardess, artist, translator. The following is typical:

Martina Wurl

The vocation of nursery teacher is very interesting. No one pays much attention to them but still they really do their duty. From morning until evening they work untiringly and take care of the children. They carry a big responsibility. They must see to it that the children get their bottles, are dry and generally well taken care of. You can learn a lot in such a job. If you don't consider the pay, nursery teachers really are rewarded. A person can select this job only if he wants to serve other people.

Fifth graders are encouraged to begin serious consideration of vocational possibilities. Their teacher, Herr Reuter, feels it is a logical time to begin an informal program of vocational counseling since, except for those few students who will transfer to a *Gymnasium,* they will have to make a vocational choice in three years. So Herr Reuter displays pictures of different occupations and takes time to discuss the demands and requirements of each.

Herr Reuter, whose wife teachers the first grade, is almost totally immersed in the life of the school, particularly his class. The couple are in their middle thirties, have no children, and occupy an apartment on the third floor of the school building. Herr Reuter has already had this class for two years and he hopes to be able to carry it through the eighth grade. He pictures himself and his wife as substitute parents for the members of the class and often speaks of the teacher's responsibility for the total growth of the pupils. Consequently, his administration of classroom activity is surrounded with a rationale somewhat democratic and idealistic in its orientation. His hyper-articulated commitment to the teaching profession is manifested in a thoroughness that overlooks few opportunities to instruct pupils in appropriate behavior. His style of teaching is not appreciably different from that displayed by the entire faculty, but his commitment is conveyed both to pupils and to their parents. The result is a sense of attachment on the part of pupils and a feeling of appreciation on the part of parents.

Subject matter is rendered in detail and periodically injected with practical and personal considerations relevant to Herr Reuter's own experiences and interests. With the fifth grade, a general course in *Heimatkunde* is replaced by separate instruction in history, civics, geography, and general science. In geography, for example, a lesson on the topography of the region involves mapwork on mountains and rivers. Pupils copy in their geography notebooks data he writes on the blackboard about the heights of nearby mountains. They accumulate and memorize much of this kind of data. The textbook, which includes history, geography, and general science, provides a general treatment of such material. Like other teachers, Herr Reuter brings much material to the class. He exploits opportunities to personalize the subject matter. In this case, the material on mountains leads to a lecture on hiking in the mountains, safety rules to follow, procedures to use in case of an accident, and accounts of his own hiking experiences.

Music education is given emphasis in all the classes. By the fifth grade, the pupils have acquired a remarkable repertory of songs which they know by heart and can sing with a lyrical quality that is admirable. Since music is one of Herr Reuter's primary interests, fifth graders experience an intense exposure to it. He has organized for the community a children's choir, and the majority of its members come from his class. He sets aside a maximum number of class hours for musical instruction, which is not limited to singing. Rhythm instruments, for example, are used in his and several other classes. The instruction is detailed: Herr Reuter spent most of one period refining a single phrase. School traditions offer many opportunities for group singing. One or two songs are always sung at the beginning and end of the day. When a pupil has a birthday, it is a custom to select two songs for the class to sing.

Religious instruction is carefully organized, rendered both formally, through normal academic procedures, and informally, through celebrations during the year. The Evangelical minister, Pfarrer Riedel, and the Catholic priest, Pfarrer Kurtz, have regular instruction with most of the classes each week for one hour. The teachers are responsible for at least one additional hour of instruction during the week, the content of which is minutely outlined in the state course of instruction. Memorization of prayers, hymns, and Bible verses is stressed. Regular homework is assigned and traditional recitation procedures are followed. In these matters, religious instruction is no different from any other class. Meaning is experienced primarily through celebrations. Since the time of our visit was early December, the beginning of the Advent season, the whole school was immersed in Christmas activities. Advent wreaths were made and hung, colorful paper designs were mounted on the windows, moments of celebration and worship were organized. On the Monday morning following Advent Sunday, a new candle in the class wreath was lit. The classrooms were darkened and each pupil had a candle to light. Christmas songs were sung and prayers offered.

Like the other teachers, Herr Reuter is firm and tolerates few deviations from orderly, attentive behavior. He does not believe in what he calls *schwache Erziehung* [permissive education], and he views with regret and some consternation the *weiche Welle* [soft wave] that is "sweeping" toward Germany from the United States. Consequently, as a substitute parent, he is as stern a disciplinarian as most parents could wish. He can very smoothly interrupt a lecture or explanation to admonish a student. If the noise level rises, he slaps the desk or yells at the class sharply.

Administering physical punishment is not difficult if the teacher is close to the pupil. If several pupils are involved and situated at different parts of the room, punitive action becomes awkward but not insurmountable. After one recess, as we were entering the room, Herr Reuter upbraided three girls for disorderly behavior. Two of them were close by; one he pulled by the hair and the other he managed at the same time to pull by the ear—all the time scolding them angrily. The third was across the room. But his sense of justice prevailed. He strode through the aisles mumbling to himself, and when he reached her desk, he twisted her ear. The room became quiet and in a few minutes the class was absorbed in a humorous story he was narrating.

Sixth grade. As early as the second grade, specialization among the teachers begins. Although the employment process makes no provisions for balancing special academic interests and talents within a faculty—since elementary school teachers are expected to be able to teach all subjects through the eighth grade—the Rebhausen faculty worked out a swapping arrangement, more or less adjusted to their special interests. Herr Könecke and Frau Boettcher teach arithmetic to other classes, Herr Kost teaches music and science to other classes, Herr Greiner branches out in drawing, Herr Doering in music and religion.

The sixth grade has two teachers, Herr Doering and Herr Greiner. As principal, Herr Doering's teaching load is reduced by half. As assistant principal, Herr Greiner's load is lightened by several hours. So they divide the sixth grade schedule according to their own interests. For the pupils, it is an experience in two markedly contrasting styles of teaching.

Herr Doering's role as principal affords and requires from him a broad perspective on village life and the problems and changes attendant to the process of industrialization occurring in the village. At the same time, his responsibility for the internal administration of the school affords him constant interaction with the interests and problems of the pupils. For these reasons—and because of his personality—his teaching style is characterized by a certain patience and understanding. He seldom raises his voice in class; he is also attentive to all the rules of behavior that other teachers enforce, but with a quiet persistence that generally lacks any sense of crisis or anger. The occasions when he has to punish a student severely are rare—usually consisting of grabbing a boy by the shoulders and shaking him roughly.

His primary academic interests are civic education and music, but he also teaches arithmetic and history. The material he utilizes in civics is especially indicative, not only of his estimate of the students and what he thinks they should understand of village life, but also of their own general demeanor and performance capacity. It has been said that Rebhausen natives are *schwerfällig* [reserved], and the teachers make the same comment about the native children. They are not less intelligent, but simply *schwerfällig*—slow to react, to formulate answers, and to express themselves without shyness in a formal situation. Consequently, Herr Doering has to pull from them slowly and somewhat painfully reactions to or ideas about the subject under discussion.

In preparing to write an essay on health he draws from them, with some prompting, the following outline.

1700	*1965*
Man believes in magic.	Man believes in medicine.
Healing herbs.	Medicine.
Very few doctors.	Many doctors.

They write, and when they are through he reads a few to the class. Some are poor, he remarks; others are good examples.

On subsequent days they discuss how boys should behave toward girls and women. (Herr Doering gave them situations to consider such as a boy sitting down in a crowded street car when a girl or a woman climbs on.) He asks them to consider what they would do if a window in the classroom were broken while he was out of the room. Some say they ought to tell the teacher who did it; others insist the class should stick together and agree not to tell the teacher. Herr Doering asks them, "What do I mean when I say that if a window is broken the whole class is responsible?"

A girl raises her hand. "The whole class has to pay."

"Not exactly," Herr Doering replies. He calls on a boy.

"It means the class behavior in some way helped bring about the broken window."

"That's better. Remember," Herr Doering goes on, "when something happens and a lot of you are involved, you must stop and work together to figure out a solution. You shouldn't always run to the teacher to tell him who did it."

It is not the first time a teacher has cautioned pupils against tattling. Most teachers seem conscious of the tendency and express interest in keeping it at a minimum. At the same time, some of the primary disciplinary devices used, in the lower grades in particular, exploit the tendency of young children to tell on each other—and make public denouncement quite respectable. Students learn that this behavior comes to be, in the later years of elementary school, unacceptable.

Herr Doering works skillfully to give students meaningful musical experiences. The sixth grade sings well. Most of the songs are either related to community celebrations, religious or secular, or to the on-going life of the community. They spend considerable time on *"Das Bauernjahr,"* a beautiful canon with text and musical response, which renders a monthly account of the farmer's primary concerns.

Herr Greiner is a different kind of teacher, but for the students interesing and certainly entertaining. He has been teaching in Rebhausen for over twenty years. Like Herr Doering and his family, he and his wife live in an apartment in the school building. Their children are grown and married. Herr Greiner is short, with angular features and a moustache that gives him more the appearance of a businessman than a teacher. He is well traveled and well read—good company among his colleagues. But he has a detached way about him, and a tendency to be totally absorbed in what he is saying. Distractions must be pronounced for him to react. Therefore, the noise level in his classroom is rather high, and the students find it possible to engage in shenanigans that in other classrooms are dealt with immediately. Accompanying his lectures is a constant buzz, as students in different parts of the room carry on conversations. When he is writing at the board, the boys spring into action. They poke each other, crawl under the desks, and concoct other distractions. When it gets too bad, Herr Greiner takes action. He removes his wrist watch from the right to the left hand (a sign students have come to recognize as ominous) so that he can slap a boy more soundly. If that is not called for, he usually pulls his hair or twists his ear.

He teaches them geography, drawing, and German, in an atmosphere that is, functionally speaking, a valuable release for this class. The rest of the school finds amusement in the stories emanating from the sixth grade classrooom.

Seventh grade. Herr Schenke, the seventh grade teacher, is thorough and knowledgeable. He is a careful student of history and political developments, well informed in all the subjects for which an elementary school teacher is responsible and forceful in his discipline. His teaching techniques reflect a carefully formulated point of view about teaching—one that is compatible with the philosophy which permeates the school and with the authority imposed from above by the state and projected into the school by the family.

A mastery of factual knowledge is basic to this point of view. Elementary school children are considered too young to evolve meaningful opinions and ideas about the more controversial aspects of political and economic developments of a historical or contemporary nature. Furthermore, the evolution of personal opinions and ideas is to be preceded by a mastery of relevant facts, a process which necessarily continues into later adolescence. Consequently, the primary obligation of the teacher is to present the facts and carefully organize learning procedures to insure their mastery. Since knowledge is such a basic measure of success, the body of material selected by the Ministry of Education (with some possibilities of modification by the teacher) has a particular significance. The teacher has a marked investment in the process, in terms not only of his reputation but also, in a more immediate sense, in the time and effort he expends distributing this knowledge to students, for example through dictation and extensive use of the blackboard. The tradition of a teacher having a class for several years compounds the investment and gives the process of mastery a longitudinal quality. Facts students learn, poems they memorize are not to be forgotten from one year to the next; consequently, review and reinforcement are important teaching techniques. The whole process, and possible deviations from it, is well illustrated in the lessons Herr Schenke develops.

A good example is the history lesson on Marxian ideology. Having assigned the students material on Marx in the textbook and lectured on it during the course of the previous week, Herr Schenke begins one day to evolve a summary which they can write in their notebook. He solicits from them key words or thoughts which have been studied thus far. The students make suggestions and he writes the key word on the board or substitutes a more appropriate word, which he first explains. When the process is completed, the following outline has been developed:

1. Economic system.
2. Classes: a) Capitalists, b) Proletariat.
3. Revolution.
4. Workers of the world, unite!
5. Religion is the opiate of the masses.
6. Destruction of private property.
7. All property belongs to the people.

Herr Schenke then spends about fifteen minutes explaining some of the inconsistencies in the doctrine and the delusive influence it had on workers who could not recognize its illogical premises. The last fifteen minutes of the period are devoted to a summary—of the summary. He calls on students to summarize the discussion, using the words and phrases on the board. The weaker students fumble and cannot put a coherent exposition together. Herr Schenke calls on one of the better students, who performs acceptably. The weaker students are asked to try again. Afterwards they all write the summary in notebooks.

Several days later when history comes up again in the schedule, the first half of class is devoted to another kind of review. Herr Schenke has written in a corner of the blackboard a series of dates which he leaves there permanently. They are: 150 B.C., A.D. 250, 476, 492, 732, 800, 843, 870, 933, 955, 962, 1077, 1120, 1190, 1254, 1273-91, 1356, 1410, 1453, 1492, 1517, 1524-1525, 1618-1648, 1632, 1683, 1740-1786, 1776, 1789, 1806, 1814-1815, 1834. The study of history has carried the class through the middle of the nineteenth century and these are dates he feels they should know. From time to time they review the dates. The better students can recite them all without a mistake.

A third form of review he uses to maintain continuity from year to year involves a question-and-answer session. A student is selected to sit at the front of the room, to answer ten questions from the class. The questions can be about anything the class has studied in the past two years. The student is graded on the number of correct answers he gives. Questioners are to know the answers to the questions they ask. One boy violated the rule. Herr Schenke's response was "Don't ask what you don't know; it's not nice." In the course of the period one day some of the questions asked were:

1. Who was Robert Koch?
2. When was the Baroque Period?
3. When did the Germanic tribe immigration begin?
4. Who was the father of the German railroad?
5. What does NATO mean?
6. What is the value in DM of the Nobel Prize?
7. Who was Marco Polo?
8. What is the insignia of the Hohenzollerns?
9. When was the American Revolution?
10. What were the causes of the increase in farm production in the nineteenth century?

As part of civics, which is scheduled one hour every two weeks, he has each student bring in a newspaper item. They are to study the item, know all the words in it, and then read it to the class. They are to be prepared to answer questions about it from other students, questions not about the implications of the item but about word meanings. For these sessions he has the study tables moved into a large rectangle to encourage face-to-face discussion. He tries to create an informal atmosphere and tells the students to stay seated when they recite. But habit is powerful; they keep standing to recite and he keeps telling them to stay seated. At the end of one such period, a news story provokes a comment by Herr Schenke about the revolution of 1848 and the great figures who attended the Frankfurt Assembly. He asks the class if they remember a poem they had learned last year, written by one of the poets at the Assembly. At least three students do, and one girl recites flawlessly and with feeling a poem by Arndt. Her performance represents a standard and medium of achievement basic to the life and program of the school. Although she is an above-average student, her classmates are in varying degrees also capable of such a performance. A formal, public rendition of ordered, discrete knowledge had been regularly demanded of them throughout their years in the *Volksschule* [elementary school]. Poetry, song, and aphorisms are the customary forms through which a kind of knowledge is shared that has not only utilitarian value for the student in the school setting, but also cultural and social value for the student as a present and future participant in the life of the community.

The account of classroom life presented in this chapter reinforces the long-established characterization of the German teacher as *König im Klassenzimmer* [King in the classroom]. The pattern of discipline reflects a markedly authoritarian implementation of teaching responsibilities. There is little deviation form this pattern; where it exists, it seems more ideological than real. The use of physical punishment, shame, public denunciation, and peer censorship to affect in the classroom acceptable behavior and academic performance are widely shared instructional and disciplinary devices. The prevailing teaching style is one which maintains the teacher in the center of classroom activity, directing, telling, correcting, judging. The primary nonacademic activity in which teachers and pupils are involved is music; here, too, the teacher's role is authoritarian. Thus as agents of cultural maintenance, teachers perform both a unifying and an isolating function. Because they share and impose rigorous standards of memorization and subject-matter mastery, they are as a group and as individuals important instruments of socio-cultural unity. Because they share and impose unilaterally rigorous standards of behavior, they are instruments of social isolation. The student must accustom himself to a public accounting of his mistakes or misdemeanors in which he stands alone, defenseless before the exercise of power.

The question may be asked: How do students react to this experience? The reality of the adjustment they make to the classroom experience is elusive. One might assume that avenues of emotional release are required to balance the heavy weight of authority. There are behavior patterns which appear to be compensatory in their function: the instances of crying among primary children when poor grades are announced, the erratic, almost frenzied, physical activity of boys during recess, the exercise of adultlike authority and discipline by older siblings toward younger siblings, the *esprit de corps* characterizing the cooperative efforts of students to circumvent or pool homework assignments. It might even by hypothesized that there is a causal relationship between the constraining environment of the classroom and the students' common delight in nature.

These behavior patterns have a physical and social setting that is often broader than the school itself and therefore less subject to systematic observation and inquiry. Of greater significance, I came to feel, is the kind of adjustment students routinely display in the classroom—an adjustment characterized by a certain resiliency directed toward the teacher. The exercise of authority, however forceful, is neither hesitant nor obtuse. A student may protest and seek to avoid the consequences of his behavior, but the dissent he mainfests is usually short-lived; a few minutes later he is likely to be an eager participant, seeking the attentio nand approval of the teacher. This scene, enacted day after day, seems to point to authority as an unalterable norm of school life and to the teacher as both the personification of this authority and as the sole agent for release from it.

Chapter 4 is an examination of one class, the eighth grade. Attention is given not only to the life of the classroom but also to the "rites of passage" that function to direct the students toward adulthood and participation in the society for which the school has presumably prepared them.

4 / The school: a class in transition

THE EIGHTH GRADERS of Rebhausen were in their final year and had their future to consider, a vocation to choose, a school to select, an apprenticeship to locate. They also had their eight years in elementary school to remember and judge. Herr Kost, their teacher, had in the closing months assigned them a theme, "A Glance Back on Eight Years of School." This is what they said:

Georg Schneider

While I was still going to kindergarten, I was real happy that I soon could go the *Volksschule.* At that time I was just six years old and very small and thin. When in the spring of 1957 I went to take the entrance tests, the examining doctors wanted to hold me back a year. But I made it and entered the first grade. The illusion was short and the repentance was long because Herr Braun was strict. Something was always happening.

After three years when I finally reached the fourth grade, I was really happy because then I was already half way through school. But the joy was short-lived as our new teacher, Herr Schmidt, pulled us on the cheek the first day. That year went by slowly and with considerable trouble. One day we heard that in the sixth grade we'd get a new teacher. We thought, "It'll be easy with her." But we were fooling ourselves because she wasn't any pot of honey. Almost every day she gave me a box on the ear. She was often sick because she wasn't very strong. During this time we had a different teacher almost every hour and that wasn't good for our education. Every morning we looked to see if Frau Menck was there because we were happy not to have so many classes.

When we entered the seventh grade and found out we were going to have a new teacher, we were more careful about being happy about it. But the new teacher, Herr Kost, impressed us. In these last two years he made up for the poor teaching we had before. If we got on his nerves, he had his stick ready to use. So it went for eight years, and soon I'll be through. Now, as the saying goes, the trials of life are just beginning.

Birgitta Schmidt

Eight years have passed since I entered the school house for the first time, full of excitement and wonder. My mother wanted to hold me by the hand but I refused out of pride because I was now a regular pupil. Full of curiosity I marched through the corridor, always a few steps ahead of my mother. Suddenly a door opened and a big man stepped out. "That is your teacher," whispered my mother to me. I must have looked at him rather anxiously because he walked up to me smiling and asked, "Do I look so fierce?" My mother smiled at me encouragingly and suddenly my anxiousness was gone.

The teacher took me through the whole building. Afterwards he led me into a classroom where a lot of children were working with pencils and colors. So I was permitted to paint a beautiful house and when my masterwork was completed I was full of pride. But we soon settled down to work. The alphabet and the one-times-one were not so easy as playing with dolls. Often I said to my mother, "Mommy, it was a lot nicer in kindergarten." But out in the street I never let on how I felt, and we first graders just laughed at the children in kindergarten. For that the older students kidded us.

So it went, one, two, three years. In the fourth and fifth grades we got Herr Schmidt as a teacher who had the habit of pinching students on the cheek. This was, depending on how hard he did it, more or less painful and well-known in the school. He was also a specialist in *Ohrfeigen*. But he had his good sides. He liked to joke with us so the lessons were usually a little lively and interesting.

The next year brought a surprise. We got a teacher who in the truest sense of the word was a "Xanthippe." Every day we had to start out singing. Whoever wasn't paying attention got an *Ohrfeige*. I have terrible memories about this time. We're satisfied with our present teacher, and there's really nothing to criticize him about, except that he sometimes overlooks some of our dictation mistakes. But that's really to our advantage.

While the years seemed awfully long, when one looks back, they really went very swiftly. In later life we'll think back on these school days as, in spite of everything, some of the best times we've had.

For the son of a factory foreman, who had lived in Rebhausen for only four years, Werner's school experience was not so different.

Werner Heinisch

When I reached my seventh birthday my parents presented me with a satchel and the necessary school equipment. Every first grader was proud of his *Tüte*. Now life began in earnest. Each day we had to get up early and go to school all morning. But we soon got used to it. About this time we moved to Frankfurt. There I learned the really basic things. When I first started to learn the alphabet and the Lord's Prayer I didn't find it easy, so I often had to stay after school.

In Frankfurt I went to a boy's school and there it was strict. Each morning in the first period we had to show our homework and our fingers. If everything wasn't in order, the teacher used a stick on the seat of our pants, and that meant that early in the morning there were often many tears.

Then we moved to Berlin and there I had the worst time. I had a woman teacher who was so down on me that she finally put me back in the fourth grade because I was always grinning and giggling like a little child and she thought I was laughing at her.

It didn't last long and we moved again and landed in Rebhausen. Here I soon noticed that there was more humor in the class, because one noticed that wine didn't taste good just to adults. My first teacher in Rebhausen was Herr Schmidt. I got along with him well although he was good at giving switchings on the fingers. So he got me now and then, and it wasn't fun, because ten blows with a bamboo stick are not exactly pleasant. Then we got in the seventh grade, Herr Kost. Our class got along with him right away, because he wasn't too strict and that was the main thing. He was exactly what our class needed. Only in one thing was he stingy and that was field trips—when it seemed they would be too long and interfere with school. At any rate, I know out of my own experience that our teacher didn't bother too much with punishments. So in a few weeks we'll have finished this year and we'll hope that what we've learned in these years will help us in later life.

These twelve boys and twenty girls remembered in considerable detail the impressionable first few days of school—entering the school building for the first time, meeting their classmates and teachers, drawing and coloring. They were sure school was going to be a great adventure, but the first six years were disappointing. From these years they recalled most vividly teachers whose behavior was erratic and whose discipline was severe. (Rebhausen adults who were asked to reminisce about their school days shared with these eighth graders a tendency to categorize teachers, first of all, according to the discipline experienced.)

The final two years were better. The students were pleased with Herr Kost. He made them work hard and was strict, but he treated their weaknesses, foibles, and misdemeanors with a sense of humor, which created in the classroom a mutual confidence. They had entered the first grade full of joy and anticipation and were leaving the eighth grade affirming that life was beginning in earnest.

LIFE OUTSIDE THE SCHOOL

The Rebhausen eighth graders were little different from any other group of fourteen-year-olds in physical growth excepting that four of the twelve boys were over six feet tall and had physiques of high school graduates. Dress was generally no indication of the occupation or wealth of their parents, with the possible exception of those few boys whose fathers were full-time farmers and who intended themselves to go into farming. At times they came to class in overalls and heavy shoes. The standard attire was plain slacks and sport shirt.

Parents' vocation and length of residence were factors which influenced the appearances of the girls. Those from the factory housing development, and originally from the northern industrial centers, tended to wear brighter clothes and keep their hair short. Those whose parents were farmers or long-time residents of Rebhausen tended to dress in somber, plain colors. About half of these girls still had pigtails. It had been traditional that girls wear pigtails until after the confirmation ceremony at the end of the eighth grade. The removal, following confirmation, was symbolic of a transition to the threshhold of an adult life. But the tradition was dying out; the pigtails were being cut off in the lower grades or not being worn at all. In this respect, the eighth grade girls were more conservative and more closely tied to the traditional folk culture of the village than those in the lower grades.

The drab, dimly lit, bulging classrooms of the old school building created an atmosphere similar to that which many of the students experienced at home. Rebhausen had been left almost completely undamaged by the war, and of the flood of refugees from the east following the war, only a few had reached the village. Nevertheless there was a housing shortage. There always had been a shortage, by the standards the natives were now beginning to acquire, but it had been accepted as central to a way of life that remained at the susistence level and that required for maintenance a strong, extended family pattern. A three-generation household was common. It was in this environment that many of the eighth graders grew up.

In the early part of the year Herr Kost assigned them an essay on "Our House." This is what some of them described:

The eighth grade.

Ingrid Bauer

Our house was built in 1827. It goes without saying that the exterior leaves something to be desired. On many places the stucco is broken off and the brick is visible. One can enter the paved yard either through the big gate or the small door adjoining the gate. In the back of the *Hof* [farmyard]are the stables and equipment sheds. On the hay racks the fodder and straw are stored. The tractor and the wagons are kept in three sheds.

Through an arched door, under the steps leading up to the house, one goes to enter the wine cellar, where a "good drop" is stored. At the far end of the wine cellar is the entrance to a smaller cellar where fruit and vegetables are stored and kept in boxes, and other assorted containers.

At the far end of the *Hof* are some narrow steps which lead to a terrace. Along the terrace is a walk, the so-called "wash walk," because my mother hangs out the clothes there to dry. A door leads into another shed where wood and other heating material is stored.

Broad, convenient steps lead up from the *Hof* to the entrance of the house. Through the door is a hallway with doors to three rooms and the steps leading to the second story. On the first floor are the living room, my parents' bedroom and my grandfather's room, and in addition the kitchen and bath.

The upper floor is not completely built, except for the room that my sister and I share. The rest of the space is just flooring where corn, grain, and all kinds of necessities are stored and kept. Up under the roof there is an old rusted smoke chamber which isn't used any more because it is in disrepair. Along one wall is a small door opening into a storage space where everything imaginable can be found, from a two hundred year old lantern to an old spinning wheel. It's the favorite place for children. Now we've arrived at the roof and on the best intention you can't go any farther—or can you?

Max Rumler

Our two and one-half story house stands on a 10 ar (approx. 11,000 sq. ft.) piece of land. Of that 5 ar are for the garden. The house was built in 1711, and the barn around 1880. The house was renovated in 1933. The garage and the woodshed were added in 1960. The house needs to be refinished on the outside. The barns will be improved next year.

In the woodshed we keep the pigs and rabbits. In the front cellar are stored the wine casks and the fruit, in the back cellar the potatoes. When we have visitors and they come in the door on the bottom floor they see there my parents' bedroom, the living room and the kitchen.

On the second story are the children's rooms (Max has three sisters and four brothers). From there we have a good view so that on New Year's Eve we can see the fireworks in Waldstadt. On the second floor live my brother and his family.

When you go through the garage you come to the garden. The fence is covered with grape vines. From the garden there is at present a good view because the workers are building the new school house. On the terrace in the summer we have to do our homework.

The garage is full of motorbikes, motorcycles and farm equipment so that the car has to stand in the *Hof*. That isn't so bad. In the *Hof* there are places for five cars. Our neighbor puts his truck there because he doesn't have enough room. I couldn't wish for a better home because we can move so freely.

For those who lived in the new housing development, the aesthetics of new construction may have been pleasing but the living space was restrictive. The people who populated this domain were not members of the extended family or neighbors who shared the Rebhausen heritage, but strangers to each other.

Rudolf Becker

I live in a stucco, four-family apartment house. The building is two stories and was built in 1959. Our apartment is on the second floor. It has an area of 64 qm. (approximately 700 sq. ft.) for which we pay very much rent. In an apartment house one has to be very quiet. We have often been scolded by the people who live below us.

On the summy side is a balcony which can be reached from the children's room or the living room. A person can't really enjoy himself out there because the neighbors can see it so well. We have flowers on the balcony which we must water and then often something spills over and drips down below. That means unpleasantness.

In the attic we have to put buckets so that it doesn't leak through the roof because with a strong wind and rain the roof tiles become loose and let the water in. That has gone on already a whole year but it hasn't been repaired yet.

Only five of the eighth graders had not been born in Rebhausen, and of these five, two were born in neighboring villages. The other three were new to Rebhausen, emigrants from northern industrial centers. Most of the eighth graders lived in old houses. Their parents were only now beginning to use the savings of a prosperous decade for renovation. The decision to spend hard-earned savings for home improvement was not a simple one to make. The natives were accustomed to living on the edge of poverty; they knew that a decent standard of living required long hours of work and parsimonious expenditure of the cash income. Furthermore, any ostentatious display of whatever wealth a family accumulated was socially unacceptable. Consequently, one made this kind of change slowly—and concentrated on the kitchen where increased space and modern conveniences could be most easily justified.

The eighth graders were the children of farmers. Not in all cases, by any means, was farming the major source of income or the primary occupation. Only five of the fathers were full-time farmers. Other vocations represented were: auto mechanic (2), mason, textile worker, truck driver, electrician, town clerk, baker, railroad policeman, butcher, machinist, unskilled labor (4), and in the case of two widows, cleaning women. But most of the families, whatever the primary source of income, owned small plots and cultivated grapes. The income from wine production raised the standard of living beyond the subsistence level and made possible expenditures for capital investments. The cultivation of the grapes required work from all members of the family, even the young children during the harvest season. The eighth graders (with those few exceptions whose parents were landless emigrants) were deeply integrated into the traditional farm culture of the village. Almost all the boys and over one-third of the girls spent at least two hours a day in farm work, and sometimes as much as four hours.

When they were in school, their time belonged to the school. As soon as the school day was over, their time belonged primarily to the family. When the chores were completed and the evening meal finished, there was homework—at least an hour a day, but little more. Herr Kost preferred to supervise the typical homework assignments during the school day. A few of the eighth graders had a room where they could work privately. Most of them worked in the living room or the kitchen, without help from their parents. The students' study habits made help unnecessary; the content of much of the work made it unprofitable.

On weekends, at least on Sunday afternoon after church and dinner, their time was their own. Rebhausen had a movie, an old converted house where films were shown on Friday, Saturday, and Sunday nights and Sunday afternoons. Eighth graders went on the average of once a month. Five of them attended no movies;

the rather conservative worship group to which they belonged considered movies banal and objectionable—a poor way to spend one's time. For those who went, the *"Winnetou"* series, based on the novels by Karl May, was the favorite. The cowboy-Indian motif was popular with children of all ages and not a few adults in Rebhausen. Most of the eighth graders had read the novels on which the movies were based. The rendition was classical and sentimental with the two main characters, Old Shatterhand, a wandering cowboy, and Winnetou, his faithful, Indian friend, maintaining a Lone Ranger-Tonto kind of relationship. The setting was authentic enough, if one could allow for a few exceptions that the Yugoslavian landscape made necessary.

If there was a television set in the home, they watched television. About 20 per cent of the families had sets, and in those homes the average viewing time of eighth graders was about ten hours per week. Those who were less fortunate managed somehow to spend two to four hours a week in front of someone else's set. But they had other things to do. The boys rode bikes or hiked into the country, built model planes, played chess, went swimming, rode horseback. The girls read (their favorite hobby), collected pictures of film stars, took care of little children, went on hikes. They were seldom very long out of sight of their parents.

LIFE IN THE SCHOOL

The eighth grade had acquired the reputation of being a problem class, primarily in the academic sense. Their education had been disrupted by a series of teachers who were erratic in attendance or incompetent in performance. The faculty and parents were concerned abut the lack of progress the class had made. When Herr Kost reported to the school in the spring of 1963, Herr Doering assigned him the class (at that time the seventh grade) with the hope that he could change the course of their rather dismal record.

Herr Kost was young, vigorous, and athletic; he attacked his teaching responsibilities with zest and determination. He could be relentlessly demanding and hover over the class with a glowering mien that, for them, meant trouble. But he could just as easily suffuse the classroom with an infectious enthusiasm. The students liked him and worked, willingly or not.

Review had been a basic instructional emphasis throughout the grades. For Herr Kost it was mandatory, not only because of the backgrond of the class but also because of the need to prepare for state examinations. The class concentrated on arithmetic and German. In arithmetic Herr Kost wanted them to be able to perform rapid mental calculations. So fifteen minutes of every arithmetic period was taken up with *Kopfrechnen*. They practiced on this kind of exercise:

1. $480 \times 20 \times \frac{1}{3} \times 16\frac{2}{3} \times 12\frac{1}{2}$.
2. 4 percent is 1.70 DM of ———?
3. 39 DM is 30 percent of ———?
4. $12\frac{1}{2}$ of ——— is 250 DM?
5. 20 DM cost, 35 DM selling price, ——— percent profit?

German was the other basic subject. Herr Kost despaired of their ever learning to write with the clarity and correctness he felt should characterize an eighth grade performance. He considered the class to be no more than average, but however weak they were in this area, they had learned to observe and to describe what they saw and remembered, particularly when the theme was nature. He assigned them the topic, "Spring on the *Engelskrone*," with the following results:

Franz Kraske

The radiant sun awakens tired nature out of its blissful sleep, for the messengers of spring are already blooming, the snowdrops and the narcissus. Soon the cherry trees, roses and other trees and bushes light up. The countryside is like a great sea of blossoms. The animals are also awakening from their winter sleep, for the sun tempts them to come out. The fox comes hungrily out of his hole and starts his search for food. Slowly nature comes to life as the sun entices plants, animals and also people into the beautiful out-of-doors. The farmer sows the grain and prepares the soil. And people from the cities travel or walk in the beautiful splendor of spring.

Martina Holm

The sun spreads its warm rays over the sleeping nature. Awakened by this warmth the first messengers of spring sprout in the meadows. The crocus stretches its violet head wonderingly toward the heavens. In the garden the *Goldregen* spreads out its colorful blossoms. The narcissus signals the beginning of spring. The brightly colored butterflies glide from blossom to blossom. Almost majestically the queen of the flowers unfolds her leaves.

Across the meadows the white shimmering blossoms of the cherry trees sparkle. In the distance one can hear the cuckoo call. The finch whistles its "Pink-epink," and all the other birds join in the song. And the field mouse dares once more to come out of his hole. In the forest the squirrel scurries like a shadow from tree to tree. In the gardens and fields busy hands are at work. The little children lie under a tree because spring has made them tired. Softly the wind breathes through the open window and brings a harmonious odor of blossoms.

When I started observations in the eighth grade, the class was studying the play, "William Tell," by Schiller. Herr Kost assigned parts and they began to read. He interrupted frequently to get them to read with more expression. Toward the end of the period, he stopped work on the play and asked them to practice a poem by Schiller, *"Das Lied von der Glocke."* They had memorized the poem in the seventh grade and he wanted them to relearn it, to know it thoroughly before the end of the year. When they finished work on the poem, he asked them to identify passages and phrases in the poem that had become a part of the folklore. His emphasis on this kind of memory work was directed, he told me, not only toward an appreciation of poetry but also toward the development of a body of common knowledge: in this case, proverbial and metaphorical expressions which were, he felt, important elements in the life of the people.

Essays I had already read, in this and other grades, offered evidence of this emphasis (conversations with adults were liberally sprinkled with such expressions). I asked him if he would test the class on the number of proverbial or metaphorical expressions they could identify. He set aside a period for the experiment and began by describing incidents or situations for which they were to find an appropriate saying. In the second half of the period, he told them to continue by simply listing all the sayings they knew. The lists numbered no fewer than forty-five and as many as eighty-six. They included the following:

1. *Er schlägt alles über einen Leisten.* [He is not very discriminating.]
2. *Der hat nicht mehr alle Tassen im Schrank.* [He's kind of crazy.]
3. *Der krug geht so lange zum Brunnen, bis er bricht.* [You can get away with something only so long.]
4. *Probieren geht über Studieren.* [Practice makes perfect.]
5. *Er läuft herum, wie die Katze um den heissen Brei.* [He doesn't face up to the problem.]
6. *In der Kürze liegt die Würze.* [Be concise.]
7. *Die Sonne bringt es an den Tag.* [The truth comes out sooner or later.]

With almost eight years of elementary school behind them, the students had accumulated an impressive fund of literary and folk sayings—a useful shorthand for defining behavior they encountered and problems they confronted. The mastery of such sayings reflected not only a specific emphasis which teachers such as Herr Kost placed on the activity, but also a general emphasis in all classes on the memorization of carefully ordered learning material. The exploration through discussion of the social, political, or personal meaning of literature such as William Tell was not a part of the students' classroom experience. Consequently, literature tended to orient them toward the past rather than the future. It was an aspect of school life they could share with adults in the community; it did not encourage habits of exploration and analysis useful in confronting the new and unpredictable developments that industrialization was bringing Rebhausen.

Civic education was not one of Herr Kost's primary interests. What he did cover was dictated more by the outline notebook he had the students purchase than by his own predilections. The notebook was divided into major topics: cooperatives, the constitution, taxation, with blank spaces for the students to fill in. Herr Kost filled it in for them—he brought to the class and lectured on material designed to fill in the outline. The procedure was straightforward: As he lectured, he had one of the students copy his notes on the board.

Essays the students wrote included "The Rights and Duties of a Citizen." It was one of several he had them write in class. They were given an hour to look for ideas in the German constitution, the history texts, and the civics notebook, and two hours to write. First came a draft, which he quickly glanced through to make major corrections, and then the final copy in ink. Herr Kost was lukewarm about the results. I had asked him if the eighth grade could write an essay on the general subject of citizenship. He felt the subject was more appropriate as a final theme at the end of three years in an advanced secondary school—a level to which only three of the eighth graders aspired. Two examples follow:

Alfred Mans

Recently I was watching a pike swimming about. When, however, it darted at a little fish, grabbed it between the teeth and swallowed it, it started me thinking on the Middle Ages. What is the connection between this scene and the world of that day and time? The farmer had to serve the noble and dance to his pipe. If "the little man" didn't want to dance, what then? He would be taken before a judge and made a slave or condemned to death. Did the farmers have no rights to defend themselves? No, they had none. How nice it is for us today in contrast. Supposing, for example, that the mayor makes a lot of noise near us on Sunday just to disturb our peace, because he figured, as the highest ranking official in the village, he could get away with it. But he would have bitten off more than he could chew because on Monday my father would go to the civil court and lodge a complaint about the disturbance of the peace based on a violation of the second article of the constitution.

The constitution was designed by a parliamentary committee for our welfare. But what would it be like if we didn't have it? It would be either a dictatorship, a monarchy or a people's republic.

But where there is light there are shadows. It's less nice naturally that we have to pay taxes. But then one has to ask immediately, "How would the streets be built and the schools, how would the post office, the railroad and the teachers be supported?" Many would say, "All of us." But what would happen without a government to organize all of this? No one would pay! But one thing is wrong, that the government pays out too much to support the armed forces. Naturally it would be dangerous not to defend the country. For that reason the tour of duty ought to be more severe but shorter.

Magdalena Graf

Haven't we all often considered why really there are laws, ordinances, requests, decrees, judges, and police? Isn't life possible without these rather unpleasant things? Now when we think back on the first men, a person could feel that we could do it that way. They lived alone in a great world and didn't need laws and regulations. Justice and injustice weren't an issue because these developed only when more people began to live together.

In a nation without justice a man cannot live securely. For each person to be assured freedom and protection rules have to be passed in which much is allowed and forbidden. Not only theft, breaking in a house, assault, and murder but also reckless driving must be punished. And for that a nation needs police and courts which can prevent and mediate controversies.

That there have been laws for thousands of years, everyone knows. There are the Ten Commandments that Moses gave to his people. When we speak of them we don't think immediately of law and right. Nevertheless they are in no way simply religious rules but they are also closely connected to legal rules.

Large societies form a state. In the Constitution of the Federal Republic it is stated that, "all the power of the state stems from the people." That means the people chose their representatives to the legislature. If a citizen is not satisfied with the enactments of the legislature, he can protest against it. He also has the right to lodge claims and complaints. This is guraranteed in Article 5. Every person has the right to express his opinion in oral, written or picture form, insofar as he doesn't injure some one else.

But it wasn't always this way. During the Third Reich people experienced just exactly the opposite. Whoever said something against the government was arrested. This sort of thing happens today under dictatorships. Hitler also acted illegally when he had the Jews gassed and condemned without a trial. In Article I of the Constitution it states: "The worth of the individual is inviolable." In Article 3 it states: "All men are equal before the law. No one is permitted to be persecuted because of sex, origin, race, religious or political convictions."

It also makes no difference whether it's a man, woman or child, whether white, black, yellow, or red, whether European or Jew—each has the same right to be defended in court. Even as little children we have this right.

The older we grow the more rights we have, but also the greater are the duties which are laid upon us. We must go to school to learn, in order that the state has an educated citizenry to be able to employ. If we earn more money, we must pay taxes. With this money the state builds streets, bridges, and hospitals and also supports schools, railroads, and the armed forces. When a citizen sometimes feels that the system of taxation is unjust he should always have the proverb in mind: *"Allen Leuten recht gatan, ist eine Kunst, die niemand kann."* [Perfect justice for all people is impossible.]

Common to most of the essays was an emphasis on the contrast between the rights enjoyed under the present government and the conditions of servitude which previous generations had experienced under serfdom, monarchies and dictatorships. Students identified the provisions in the constitution concerned with basic rights and took note of the relationship between rights and civic responsibilities. They mentioned the more immediate and sometimes painful obligations which the present government laid upon them—or their parents and older brothers. There could be little question about the ability of these eighth graders, products of a rural environment who are destined one day to join the broad, lower middle class of German society, to expostulate cogently on the structure and function of democratic government. There is less reason to be assured of their future ability to handle the functional, interpersonal relationships required to maintain the vitality of democratic government.

Appropriate civic education in the *Volksschule* is confronted with a dilemma rooted in structural arrangements and pedagogical predilections. The conviction among the teachers that growth patterns of elementary school children necessarily impose limits on a program of civic education has a logical basis. They submit that it is delusive to play at democracy in the school when children are so young, inexperienced, and intellectually immature. The primary assertion is simply that facts must precede opinion and analysis. The problem is not alone that, given this assumption, the process of acquiring facts can continue endlessly, since the body of facts is endless. That was a problem in the Rebhausen school. But structural arrangements in the educational system add a more significant dimension to the problem. These eighth graders are at the threshold of the adult world, and their next school experience will have an overriding vocational orientation. Consequently, the elementary school, practically speaking, is the last educational institution that can be totally concerned with the general education of the students. The question becomes, regarding meaningful civic education, if not now, when?

The problem, in all its fragile, contradictory characteristics, becomes particularly vexatious when the treatment of the Nazi period is considered. Herr Kost and others on the faculty had recognized the problem but had found no satisfactory solution. It was, he said, a difficult period to teach. Older teachers had had to join the Nazi party. For them to develop a meaningful study of the period was especially unsettling. (Their problem became, in part, his.) The subject, he observed, was also not very popular with parents. Furthermore, he felt textbooks were inadequate; there was insufficient attention to the German side of the question. Finally, the subject was too complex for the students to understand. Consequently, his treatment was cursory, factual as far as the basic events of the period were concerned, shallow as far as any analysis was concerned. When, for example, he showed them a series of films on the period, there was no discussion following the films, only a few questions by Herr Kost about certain facts. He had them consider the whole period in an essay, *"Bilanz eines Weltkrieges"* [An Evaluation of World War II].

Werner Heinisch

The greatest horror of this last world war was the persecution of the Jews. These five million Jews all Germans have on their conscience today. Hitler and his henchman, Eichmann, and Germany will never be forgiven for this murder and torture. Still it shouldn't be forgotten that in the second world war at Stalingrad around 200,000 German soldiers fell at the front. Now the war really began in Germany.

The English and the Americans destroyed almost all of the large cities. Hunger and misery came to the nation. Almost all Germans were without shelter; they lived in cellars and ruins. The German people grew weaker.

The English, French, Americans, and Russians took large areas of land from the Germans. Today we still hope for a reunification with middle Germany and that the area behind the Oder-Neisse Line will once more belong to Germany.

If we were ever to think that a war would be useful, we only need to consider the past. Then we would have to understand how senseless and brutal this war was. The consequences were that we had to pay big reparations. Now we hope that war will never break out again. That's the wish of each German.

Lisa Hamel

In 1933 when Hitler came to power he gave the German people much hope. He established himself as leader and chancellor. He promised work for 7 million Germans. For that reason he got many followers. But the Germans soon noticed what Hitler had in mind. He outlawed all parties except the NSDAP. In brown shirts the party leaders marched and traveled on trucks through the country organizing meetings.

The Jews were for Hitler a thorn in the eye. He counted them as semitic. He couldn't see that the Jews were excellent businessmen. He had thousands of them and other people put in concentration camps. They were crowed together,

10,000 to 30,000 in small camps. Innocent women, children, and men received "special treatment." They were slowly tortured to death. In many camps they were gassed. At the end of this period millions had lost their lives through gassing, shooting, and starvation. It is even today for us Germans a terrible shame.

On the 22nd of June, 1941, Hitler marched without a declaration of war into Russia. It was supposed to have been a blitzkrieg like in France. But Hitler fooled himself. Russian soldiers were defeated and great numbers taken prisoner. Hitler believed then that he had won the war, but the Russian winter came too soon. The German soldiers had no warm clothing and they lacked weapons. The Russians counterattacked. Of the 330,000 German soldiers fighting there only 90,000 returned home. Now the Germans see that this war was senseless. Hopefully there will never be such a war again.

The summing-up reflected not only what they heard in the classroom but also the feelings their parents and other adults in the village expressed about events of this period: the unrest and unemployment leading to Hitler's rise to power, the tyranny of the regime, the horror of the Jewish persecution, the attack on Russia and the disaster at Stalingrad, the postwar misery and the loss of territories, and finally, the futility of war.

CHOOSING A VOCATION

For people of the soil, traditional life in Rebhausen had, like the seasons of the year, a fixed and reassuring rhythm. The celebration of birth, the awakening experiences of early childhood, the restraining demands of school, the years of vocational training, marriage and work—work until one was too feeble to go into the fields or to wield the tools of a craft. The rhythm was sustained and renewed by generation after generation. Few natives left the community to seek a more satisfying life elsewhere.

Through the years subsistence depended on the efficient participation of all members of the extended family. For girls that meant that the most utilitarian vocational training they could choose was home economics—two years in a school in a nearby city and then work at home. They lived at home while attending school, not only because they were needed but also because the vocational program required both formal schooling and practical experience. For boys the obligation was clear. They chose their father's vocation, attended a vocational school one day each week for three years, and worked the rest of each week under the tutelage of their fathers. The process of renewal was simple and unending.

Eighth graders preparing to leave the elementary school had traditionally considered few alternatives. That they would live in Rebhausen and work their father's land or learn his craft was a foregone conclusion. The economic necessity was reinforced by other traditions and conditions. The elementary school education was, practically speaking, terminal, in the sense that at its completion students had to commit themselves to a particular vocation. When the time came to marry and establish a home, young people knew they would probably marry someone in the village.

Leaving the community to marry or bringing in an outsider was viewed with considerable opposition—an affront to the belief that the village itself was capable of providing for all the necessities and desires of life.

But the rhythm of renewal is being disrupted. War has decimated a generation of males. Prosperity and the factory have created a new mobility, a changing pattern of vocational possibilities, and an exposure to the good things of life, which customarily have not been found in Rebhausen. Consequently, eighth graders had to make infinitely more complicated vocational choices; they had to balance their own rising aspirations against the deeply entrenched traditions of their parents.

An organized program of vocational counseling begins late in the seventh grade with a visit to the school by a representative of the state employment office. He comes to talk to parents about the conditions of employment and the kinds of vocational training and education for which their children may be eligible. The presentation he made to those parents who attended (eleven women, three men) was broad and flexible in its rendition. He proposed to parents that they respect the vocational interests of their children and allow them the privilege of contemplating different vocations, until they found one they really liked. Interest and aptitude were, he suggested, the paramount criteria for making an intelligent decision. Aptitude had three aspects: physical qualifications, intellectual qualifications, and character—that is, persistence, patience, and sensitivity in human relations.

He described the kinds of schools for which their children might be eligible, one of which they would have to attend. The spectrum of vocational training possibilities was broad; the presentation indicated an understanding of the problems attendant to the process of making a choice. But eighth graders were almost unanimous in expressing discontentment with the vocational counseling they had received. The crucial point in this process occurred in the early part of the eighth grade, when the employment office representative returned to counsel individual students. Grades were carefully assessed in relationship to vocational courses. Estimates of physical capacities were made. The object of the interview was to make a final decision on a vocation. Students were confronted with a reality with which they were not prepared to cope.

In the period following the interviews Herr Kost assigned them an essay, "Why I Want to Learn this Vocation." The problems of making a choice are manifest in what they wrote.

Rudolf Becker

It won't be long until I'll be through with school. Now we're faced with a difficult question. What do you want to learn? What kind of a vocation do you want to master? When I was younger I first took it for granted that I'd learn some kind of vocation. But it's only now that I understand what this new phase in my life means. Because my grades aren't very good, I can't go on to a secondary school. My dream was always to be a captain. I was also interested in being an electrician and a pilot. But I don't think about that anymore, because my grades aren't good enough. So I have decided to become an auto mechanic.

I find this vocation interesting because I prefer to work with machines rather than with pencil and paper. It's certainly not a clean vocation but I can expect plenty of work because the auto has a good future. To be sure I hope that I can continue my education so that I don't remain an auto mechanic all my life. The work of a machinist is still out of the question for me due to health reasons. Still the vocation has its advantages. For example, a person can build up a little business or travel to other parts of the country and assemble machines.

But it's hard work. So I'm going to learn to be a mechanic. Hopefully in this job I'll become a rich and successful person.

Elfriede Spierling

After school is out, life will really begin in earnest. When I was younger I thought often about what kind of vocation I really wanted to learn. When I started to school, I intended to become a kindergarten teacher, because I had much fun taking care of little children. When I grew older and wiser, I recognized that I wasn't suited to this vocation because I no longer had the patience and nerves for it.

Then I came to the idea that I could become a druggist. I considered for awhile. As I thought about the decision, I asked a druggist to tell me about prescriptions. When the teacher asked me one day what I wanted to learn I gave him this answer, "I'd like to become a druggist." But he advised me against it.

Now comes the time when I have to make a decision. I asked my mother for advice. But she said, *"Wer die Wahl hat, hat die Qual"* [It's hard to make a choice]. Now I've made a decision, to go to Waldstadt as a saleswoman. I hope this vocation will please me later on.

For many eighth graders the *"Ernst des Lebens"* began late in March when they reported to the vocational school and to their apprenticeship employer. Of the twelve boys in the class three had qualified for further full-time schooling, two for intensive two-year courses in commercial subjects and business machine repair, and the third for a three-year course leading to the *Mittlere Reife* [intermediate school certificate] and commercial work. The latter, a bright, energetic son of the village clerk, was contemplating pushing on to the *Abitur* [Final high school and college matriculation examination] and teaching, if he proved successful in this course.

The other nine had chosen, or were forced to choose, the more traditional route, that is, two to three years of part-time vocational school combined with apprentice-ship training at some business. The apprenticeships were distributed as follows: auto mechanic (3), sales apprentice (3), farming (2), and gas-water installer (1). The two who had chosen farming were apprenticed to their fathers. Of the other seven, two had apprenticeships in Waldstadt and five in Rebhausen. One student was an apprentice at the chemical factory where his father worked.

Several months after graduation, I called the class together to talk about their experiences and to compare this new life with what they had left behind in school. Rudolf Becker, the boy who finally and reluctantly decided to become an auto mechanic, had this to report:

My apprentice employer is an automobile concern in Waldstadt. I attend school two mornings a week and the rest of the time I am at the auto concern.

In school I am studying arithmetic, German, drawing, religion, business economics, and engine mechanics. My main job at the concern is to bring tools to the mechanics and help with the light work.

The biggest difference between life in the elementary school and at the concern is the conscientiousness with which I must perform my work here. What I like best about it is working together with the other apprentices and the journeymen. Then too because I have to go to Waldstadt each day I have opportunities to meet my old school comrades, at least those who also take the train each day.

What I don't like is having to get up early each day and then come home late. The concern sells new cars which must be specially washed to protect the finish. So from time to time each apprentice must go to the wash rack and help the Spanish workers wash the cars. I don't like to do that either because the work is very dirty, as anyone can imagine.

I don't find much difference between my former teachers and my present boss, only that the boss gives me more work to do. Homework from the vocational school takes much of my time. My present teacher there is strict and we really have to pay attention. For any damage in the school I have to pay part. It is an obligation to greet the teacher each day.

Of the 20 girls in the class, 3 were continuing with full-time schooling. One of them had qualified for an *Aufbaugymnasium* and was planning to be an elementary schoolteacher. She was the outstanding student in the class and had given the class oration at graduation. Of the other seventeen, 10 had been placed in apprenticeships: hotel maid (3), grocery store clerk (1), department store clerk (1), hairdresser (2), bank clerk (1), factory clerk (1), bakery clerk (1). Of the remaining seven, six were attending home economics school, which were almost full-time for one or two years, and the seventh was training to be a nurse. Of the 10 who had apprenticeships, four were located in Waldstadt or more distant communities. Two of the girls had to leave home and live on the premises of their new job. The class was beginning to break up. One of the girls, who began an apprenticeship in the local bank, had this to report:

Brigitta Schmidt

I have chosen to become a bank clerk. In order to do that I have to attend a *Handelschule*. In the second year I'll be in a banking class, while in the first year I am taking general business. I attend the school two half days a week and take economics, commercial arithmetic, correspondence, German, religion, typing, and shorthand.

The rest of the time I work at the bank. My chief duties are sorting receipts of the day and mailing out the account reports. From time to time I have to run errands, polish the gold coins, and pack change in rolls.

The difference between the elementary school and an apprenticeship is to my way of thinking very big. It isn't said in vain that after the elementary school the *"Ernst des Lebens"* begins. That is not to say that the school time was only play. It's just that in my opinion in school it was more free and there was less pressure, while in my apprenticeship there's more restraint. Especially the discipline in the bank was for me at the beginning a little hard to get used to.

What pleases me especially in the bank is the personal atmosphere. I know each of the other young people working there, from school days. Among us there is a friendly, natural relationship, and that I find wonderful. It's my opinion that the good relationship among the bank officials has a great influence on the pleasant atmosphere and too on the success the bank has. So I'm pleased with my apprenticeship—and would be lying if I said I weren't.

The relationship to my boss is more personal than to my teacher. When he has to censure me (which often is necessary) he does it in a humorous way and that I find especially nice.

Homework from the *Handelschule* is generally harder than at the elementary school, but that's not surprising. Teaching methods I find are now stricter. Especially the homework is graded more severely. About discipline I can only say that during class no one is permitted to speak out of turn and you have to be punctual to class.

THE FINAL MONTH

Examinations. The students had often said that after graduation life was going to begin in earnest. It was a simple summing-up of the impending experience—a folk-saying or cliché they had learned at home, heard at school, and had come to feel was the way adults wanted them to understand the change. The final month's activities fixed the attention of the students on the transition that was taking place.

The process began late in February with state examinations. Grades, entrance tests, and interviews had been completed and the results submitted to the schools the students hoped to attend. The state test had little if any effect on the students' standing in the Rebhausen school. They were all going to graduate. If they did not, they were old enough to quit school, so there was no reason to hold them back at this point. The test was designed mainly to give the state comparative data on all elementary schools. It consisted of a dictation (one and one-half hours), arithmetic exercises (two hours), and and essay (two and three-quarter hours).

The dictation began with these directions:

> The text below is to be read to the students once by the teacher in a pace appropriate for dictation. In the process it is permitted to repeat portions of the text. Of the punctuation marks only the periods are to be dictated. At the end of the dictation the text should be read again in order that the pupil can check his work. At that point pupils have five minutes to read through their work. Requests to have single words or whole sentences repeated are to be denied.

The text was titled "Aid to Underdeveloped Nations" and follows:

> United Nations' surveys of world economic conditions show that each year more than 23 million people starve to death. Underdeveloped nations are especially threatened by famine. How is this to be explained? Among these underdeveloped countries are many former colonies of European powers. The white man educated natives about modern, sanitary public health measures. Epidemics became much less frequent, but agricultural techniques have not been keeping

pace with a rapidly increasing population. Industry is almost nonexistent. So industrial nations who enjoy a higher standard of living are providing financial support to the underdeveloped nations. Next to financial help technical help has a high priority. Scientists, technicians, and specialists are being sent as advisors. It is hoped that more modern agricultural practices will increase productivity. Handwork enterprises and small factories are being started. Where conditions are favorable, big industries are being developed. Streets and roads are being built, harbors and airports constructed, communication media expanded. The most important responsibility is to build schools in order to raise the level of education of the population. The purpose of this aid is to help these nations become more self-sufficient and eventually full and equal trading partners with us.

Correction instructions to the teacher were:

More than one mistake in the same word is to be counted as one mistake. If the student misspells the same word more than once it is to be counted as one mistake. Mistakes in syllable separation, sentence punctuation, and carelessness (forgetting to dot the "i's" or to put in the umlaut) are to be counted one-half. The evaluation key is:

Mistake	Grade
0	1
1–2	2
3–5	3
6–8	4
9–12	5
13–16	6
over 16	6

Half mistakes are to be rounded off to the benefit of the pupil.

After a half-hour recess, the eight graders returned to the classroom to work five exercises in arithmetic, an example of which follows:

Three adjacent villages decided to build a playing field which will cost 15,470 DM. 40 per cent of the cost will be paid by the state. The additional expense will be shared by the three villages according to their populations, 850, 765, and 595. How much will each village have to pay?

In correcting the papers the teacher was given the following instructions:

If a problem is correctly set up but not completed, or if it contains only one mistake, it is to be counted one-half. If the test contains only one half-completed problem, the problem is to be counted as all wrong. If the test contains 2-3 half-completed problems, these problems are together to be counted as one correct answer. If the test contains 4-5 half-completed problems, these are together to be counted as two correct answers.

On the following day the class was given almost three hours to write an essay on one of the following themes:

1. Why would you not like to live under a dictatorship?
2. Advertising puts pressure on you to buy. How do you react to it?
3. Technology helps today's housewife.
4. What should a person be like that you would like to choose as a good example to follow?
5. What can you do to realize your vocational interest?

According to Herr Kost, most of the students avoided a topic which required obvious moral judgments. They preferred writing about advertising and vocational interests.

Orientation.   Following the test the eighth graders had three weeks of school, characterized by a leisurely pace. Herr Kost continued to work on review, but he was spending much of the time preparing for graduation exercises, since the class was to play the primary role. During this period they had an eight-hour course in first aid, conducted by a Red Cross representative.

Primary attention was focused on an orientation program, *Brücke zum Leben* [Bridge to Life], organized by Rektor Doering. It had become increasingly important to him that the school prepare eighth graders more adequately for adulthood. The dramatic changes that the village is experiencing intensified the need. The program, consisting of a series of lectures and field trips, did not include all the changing experiences confronting eighth graders, but it did expose them to some of the realities of adult life.

The first lecture was by the mayor who had set aside an entire day for a review of village government. During the first hour he lectured to them on the structure and function of the government. He described his duties and interests, from the administration of the *Rathaus* staff to the responsibility for maintaining an active cultural and social life in the village. He described the police powers that belong to his office and reminded the students that the village keeps a record on all felonies Rebhausen citizens commit, whether the case occurs under local jurisdiction or in some remote city. "We can see," he said, "what Rebhausen citizens do when they leave here." He pointed out that housing is his most important responsiblity. He told them of the importance of the factory and that without it the recent improvements (streets, the swimming pool) would not have been possible. His closing observation was that village life would run smoothly only if he maintained an active interest in all aspects of it.

At the end of the lecture the mayor called for questions. Herr Kost had the normal sensitivity of a teacher about whether or not his class would perform acceptably in the presence of the mayor. When the questioning got underway, he kept prodding the students to say something, whispering suggestions to those near him. They responded and the mayor was able to expound for another hour in response to the questions.

For the rest of the day the class experienced a mock village election, which the mayor had proposed and was prepared to help them organize. He appointed an election committee to handle the normal administrative duties. The class organized itself into two parties, by sex, and each group made up a voting list of five candidates. The lists were shuttled to the *Rathaus* [town hall] and ballots mimeographed. The mayor observed that he could himself participate in a regular village election only as a private citizen, but he could ask the people to elect *anständige Leute* [upstanding citizens] with whom he could work successfully. After this speech the class voted. Most of the students kept the ballot secret, but Herr Kost could not contain his curiosity and wandered about the room to see how they were voting.

The students took the ballots to the *Rathaus,* where the election committee was set up, and deposited them in the village ballot box. The count was made and the results announced. Three boys and two girls had been elected—a revolutionary development, since in the history of the *Gemeinderat* no woman had ever been elected, or for that matter, had ever run. After the election the mayor helped them organize and conduct a meeting of a *Gemeinderat.* The main item on the agenda was the new school building.

The second lecture was by Herr Bergmann, the president of the local bank. He described the operations of the bank and its relationship to the economic life of the village—very basic but, after an hour, a strain on the attention span of eighth graders. The session became somewhat noisy before it ended. The third lecture, on county government, was delivered by Herr Schmidt, member of the county council and of the Rebhausen *Gemeinderat.*

Since the lecturers were guests of the school as well as the class, Herr Doering was usually there to introduce them. The fourth lecturer, the state representative from the Waldstadt area, was an acquaintance of Herr Doering and a former teacher. Herr Sohl's presentation ranged over a wide variety of subjects. He described the structure and operation of state government and then plunged into a discussion of some of the more vexing problems confronting the state and national government. His opening observation set the tone:

> Foreigners say we are too obedient, like to follow orders, don't think for ourselves enough. It's true. We aren't independent enough, but we should be. As you grow older, that is one of your most important responsibilities.

They discussed the housing shortage, foreign workers, the confessional schools, rising prices, foreign aid to underdeveloped countries, weapon shipments to Israel, the shortage of secondary schools that elementary school graduates can attend. Herr Kost did not have to prompt them. He had the feeling that they had already been prompted—by their parents.

During the orientation program they made two trips, one to Waldstadt to attend a court case, the other to the wine cooperative. The final lecture, *"Politik ohne mich"* [Politics without Me], was given by a radio and television writer and commentator who had taken an interest in political education for schoolchildren as well as adults. Herr Lewin built his lecture out of questions. He probed them to find out what they understood, and he learned how difficult it was to get them to participate. His primary concern was that they learn something about civic action: how complaints can be lodged against the state, what is involved in fighting a violation of the constitution, and how citizens can organize and act to change something in the community, when the government remains indifferent. He told them their motto ought to be not *Politik ohne mich* but *Politik mit mir* [Politics with Me].

Graduation. On March 26, 1965, in the Rebhausen *Turnhalle,* the eighth grade graduated. It was an important community celebration. The entire school was there, seated in one section, with the graduating class in the right front rows. The Mayor, *Gemeinderat,* faculty, and special guests were escorted to front rows on the left. Parents, relatives, and friends overflowed the rest of the auditorium.

The program reflected the interests and talents not only of the school but also of the community. There were songs by the children's choir, by a special choir of seventh and eighth graders, and by the sixth grade. There was instrumental music by a group of lower graders, a folk dance by the seventh grade girls, a poetry recitation by two small third graders, and a selection by two eighth graders. There was a play put on by the eighth grade, directed by Herr Kost. The students performed with a skill and expressiveness that was a result not only of the training they had received throughout their school years but also of Herr Kost's own vigorous approach to life.

Herr Doering spoke about the past year, the growth of the school, and the attendant problems. He praised the teachers for their work, thanked the mayor and the *Gemeinderat* for their support and interest in education, and urged parents to take a more active interest in the school. Then he turned the meeting over to Herr Kost who talked to the eighth graders, reminiscing about his two years with them, reviewing their strengths and weaknesses, recalling the fun they had had together, and urging them to perform at their best in the world they were about to enter. The outstanding student in the class responded with a short speech.

For eighth graders Herr Kost had book awards: the student with the best overall grade, the student with the best grade in arithmetic, the student with the best grade in German, the student who had kept the classroom bookcase in order, and finally the student who for two years had faithfully kept the blackboard clean. Herr Doering gave out certificates to student patrol leaders and to those who had read widely from the school library. The ceremony ended with Herr Kost handing out final report cards to the eighth graders and to those from the lower grades who were leaving the school to begin work. (One seventh grader, three sixth graders, and one fifth grader had completed the required eight years.)

At the end of the evening there were more speakers. Herr Bergmann, chairman of the parent's council, praised the teachers for their work and observed that things ran so smoothly in the school there was no need for the council to take any action. Finally, the mayor expressed to the faculty, on behalf of the community, his appreciation for their devotion to the education of Rebhausen children.

The curtains on the stage were closed and the crowd began to stand up. But the ceremony was not completed. From offstage came the eighth graders, bringing gifts to the teachers. The presentations were informal and personal as the students milled through the crowd and found the teachers. This done, the students went home; it was close to 11:00 P.M. But the faculty was not finished. It is traditional for the community to honor teachers with a meal following the exercises. The mayor, the *Gemeinderat,* and the teachers retired to a restaurant where Rebhausen wine and food was served until 1:00 A.M.

According to custom, the eighth grade returned to school the next morning to clean out their desks, straighten up the room, and say good-by. Thirty of them moved from room to room to greet and shake hands with the teachers.

Two days later a final touch was added; a class party was organized. A room in a restaurant in Buchdorf, two miles away, was reserved. There was no transportation available, so the students walked over and spent four noisy hours, talking and singing and drinking—cokes, beer, and wine. Herr Kost was the chaperone. He brought his guitar and kept the party moving. He had composed a poem, which he sang, celebrating the foibles of each student. By midnight some of them were woozy; others were just getting underway. The hike back was one long, joyful chorus of song and laughter.

Confirmation. On the Sunday following graduation exercises the twenty-six Protestant eighth graders were confirmed in the Evangelical church. Since November of the previous year they had spent one afternoon each week in a confirmation class, conducted by Pfarrer Riedel. The class was voluntary, but all of them enrolled. The tradition was basic; the community, Pfarrer Riedel felt, would have expressed disapproval had a student not participated.

The goal, he said, was to lead them into the life of the community, but the agenda was narrowly oriented toward preparation for church membership, that is, the basic doctrine and liturgy of the church. Study during the weekly sessions was intensive, with songs, Bible verses, and prayers to memorize. Pfarrer Riedel set aside time during each session for discussion but was never satisfied with the participation he managed to develop. It was, from the standpoint of the eighth graders, part of the school day.

Confirmation extended over two Sundays, the first Sunday being devoted to the examination. Two weeks before the examination, the class (Catholics excepted) spent three days at a youth hostel, to be together as a group away from familiar surroundings, to enjoy a trip they might not otherwise take (they spent Sunday in a nearby Swiss town), and to make final preparations for the confirmation services.

The purpose of the examination was to determine if the individual had sufficient mastery of the facts of Biblical literature and history to qualify for church membership. The church was crowded. The eighth graders occupied the front pews. After the sermon Pfarrer Riedel stepped down from the pulpit and examined them. Each student received at least one question. The Pfarrer tried to make certain that the poorer students would get questions they could answer.

The following Sunday they were confirmed, an important event in the life of the student and of the community. The ceremony was meant to have spiritual and social significance, and eighth graders understood it that way. Godparents, relatives, and friends gathered for a day of feasting following the service. The day after confirmation pigtails disappeared.

The confirmation tradition was a vivid reminder to eighth graders of some of the basic characteristics of the village and of village institutions which had structured their lives. The day seemed to consume the whole village, but the tradition was Protestant. Catholics received communion at the age of nine, and for them, there was no religious ceremony connected with the end of elementary school. But Catholic eighth graders did attend a one-day orientation conference in a nearby community while the Evangelical students were at the youth hostel.

The confirmation tradition was unifying as well as divisive. The confirmation class as a group included a wider social and academic representation than ever before. It consisted of those who had been in school eight years. Most of them were in the eighth grade; a few were those scheduled to leave school early. Six of the group were Waldstadt Gymnasium students living in Rebhausen, only one of whom was a native who had spent the first four years in the local *Volksschule*. The pervasive influence of the church in the life of the community had created, from students with diverse educational aspirations and vocational interests, a group which would, in the years to come, return to renew their common interest.

The final year of elementary school was for the eighth graders transitional in many respects. Their involvement in and orientation toward the life of the school was gradually disestablished and in the final month their attention was sharply directed toward civic, religious, and vocational commitments and obligations common to adult life in Rebhausen. It is appropriate to view these transitional experiences as authentic rites of passage. In most cases students chose, or were forced to choose, a vocation—one they would probably follow the rest of their lives. They were, after a long period of preparation, inducted into the church. For girls this step meant sanction to cultivate an adult appearance. The students were young, but their parents constantly reminded them that life was really beginning in earnest.

However authentic the confirmation rites may have been for this class, a question remains about their real meaning. These students were graduating from an elementary school; their average age was fourteen. They were products of a rural, unsophisticated environment and possessed all the normal interests and developmental characteristics of boys and girls that age. The commitment the traditional culture of Rebhausen imposed most emphatically on eighth grade graduates was work. The subsistence level had through the years made this necessary, and students had already been enculturated into this aspect of village life.

At the same time the organic relationship of Rebhausen to the larger, urban environment was creating among students interests relatively new to the traditional culture. These interests were beginning to be closer to those of urban youth. Television, movies, and motorbikes were making inroads into the traditional pastimes such as hiking and informal play. Consequently, the cluster of interests and activities the youth were developing are suggestive of an age level which in an urban, industrial environment precedes induction into adult society. The drama and meaning (especially that identified by the students themselves) of these rites affirm their function in the traditional life of the village; however, changes beginning in that culture and the emerging interests of the students point to a declining importance of the rites.

5 / The school: authority,
its sources and uses

THE ROLE THE SCHOOL in Rebhausen develops in transmitting the traditional culture and mediating cultural change is affected not only by the enduring life of the village and by impelling forces for change such as the factory but also by individuals, groups, and institutions whose established authority impinges on the life of the school. It is clear that an active response by the school to the kind of change Rebhausen is experiencing requires versatility and maneuverability on the part of the faculty. To assess the response the faculty is manifesting, it is necessary to consider the sources and uses of authority which have their origin outside the school.

THE FACULTY AND THE STATE

The school building belongs to the community; the teacher belongs to the state. Neither village officials nor the school principal are involved in the selection of new teachers for their community. In the teaching profession the process of closure and promotion is controlled by the state, a fact which helps to explain the local independence a teacher enjoys.

Undergraduate education for those who decide to become teachers is varied, but all candidates for elementary and junior high school teaching must eventually complete a three- year program at a teachers' college. The program is thorough, requiring work in educational theory, philosophy, theology, psychology, sociology, and all the subjects normally taught in the elementary school, as well as in the activities supervised: music, art, physical education, and handicrafts. The academic preparation is supplemented by practical experience. At the end of each of the first two semesters, student teachers spend between eight to fourteen days in a city school and are given short teaching assignments. During the third, fourth, and fifth semesters, they are to spend at least one day a week in practice teaching under the supervision of the regular teacher. Between the fourth and fifth semesters a month's experience in a rural school is required. Until recently, graduates have been required to be proficient in at least two musical instruments—now only one is required.

At the conclusion of the program, state exams must be passed to establish eligibility for a probationary teaching assignment. The standard format is a five-hour written exam in psychology and a three-hour written exam on methodology. A short oral exam completes the test program. If the student is successful, he is designated as *Beamter auf Wiederruf* [a civil servant with a provisional certification].

The college registers all prospective teachers with the *Oberschulamt* [a regional office of the Ministry of Education], and this office distributes the names to county offices designated by the candidate. The latter has some choice of assignment if his grades are good enough. It has been traditional that beginning teachers be assigned to rural schools, the rationale being that it is a valuable pedagogical experience. Furthermore, it is always harder to recruit teachers for these areas becuause of the attractions of the city. However, in making the assignment, the county office gives some consideration to the grades on the exams. A "1" may enable a candidate to avoid a rural position.

Three years of probation are required, after which a second examination is administered. In the second of these three years, the teacher re-establishes contact with a professor at the teachers' college and solicits advice in choosing a theme for a lengthy paper on some aspect of teaching. The professor is to read and grade the paper and send the grade to the *Oberschulamt*. In the first year of probation the teacher is also required to write a report on some teaching experience, and at the end of the third year, there is a short oral exam.

The climax of the probationary period is the examination by the *Oberschulrat* [county superintendent—but a state official] of the teacher's classroom performance. This teacher evaluation technique is central to understanding the teacher-pupil and teacher-community relationship. During the three years of probation the *Oberschulrat* visits the teacher at least once each year, to spend time observing, counseling, and directing. (The supervisory role of the principal remains very informal.) Since the school's schedule is on file at the county office, the *Oberschulrat* can decide in advance what classes he will observe. His arrival is not prearranged.

These interim visits are primarily for counseling, although the teacher does receive a grade. But the final visit, a formal evaluation, is perhaps the most important part of the whole process. Teachers at Rebhausen feel that the grade one receives on this examination is crucial. Although a "3" or even a "4" is considered acceptable and passing, a "2" is necessary if one wishes to teach in the city, where the competition for positions is more intense, or if one aspires to become a principal.

In addition to these considerations of subsequent job opportunities, there are many considerations relative to achieving a permanent status in the teaching profession. If, at the end of the probationary period, the teacher's total performance on tests and teaching is satisfactory, he is given a classification of *Beamter auf Lebenzeit* [permanent civil service classification]. The perquisites are considerable:

1. *Job security.* A teacher cannot be fired except for criminal behavior, moral turpitude, or gross neglect of duty. He cannot be transferred to another position without his consent (unless as a punishment established at a trial by Ministry officials). If for some reason his position is eliminated, the state is obligated to find him another position of comparable status.

2. *Remuneration.* The salary scale for teachers, once very poor, has been climbing steadily in the past decade, especially for elementary school teachers, of which there is a shortage. The beginning salary is approximately 800 DM, better than av-

erage for wages and fixed salaries throughout the state. The pension plan permits at retirement a pension equal to 75 percent of the last salary. Medical insurance, usually a combination of state and private plans, provides almost complete coverage at reasonable rates. Depending on the size of the town, teachers receive a housing allowance, averaging perhaps 100 DM per month. The community is obligated to locate inexpensive housing for the teachers.

The stakes are high. Herr Könecke was finishing his probationary status and preparing for the final requirements. While I was there, he completed his written exam and his research paper and was subjected to an evaluation of his teaching. The process began when he notified the *Kreisschulamt* [county office of education] that he was ready for the evaluation. It is generally assumed that after this registration a candidate can expect as many as five months to elapse before the evaluation. In Herr Könecke's case, a month was given to make general preparations. Eight days prior to the evaluation he was sent notification of the classes and subjects he was to teach. In his case it was arithmetic to the seventh grade, civics to the fourth grade, and German to the third grade, his own class.

The examining committee consisted of the *Oberschulrat,* an experienced teacher from a nearby village, and Herr Doering, as principal. The combined vote of the three determines the final standing, but Herr Doering explained that the position and prestige of the *Oberschulrat* gives added weight to his evaluation. Herr Doering usually reviews the record of the teacher with the other two. He wants to protect the chances of a promising but erratic teacher and also make it a little easier to get rid of a candidate who is patently incompetent.

On the morning of the evaluation there was an undercurrent of excitement within the faculty. They commiserated with Herr Könecke, talked of their own anxieties and experiences, and described the personalities of the *Oberschulräte* who had examined them. The following is an account of the first period, with the seventh grade class in arithmetic.

8:35	Könecke waits for the three to stop talking and then begins. *Oberschulrat* gets up after a few minutes and walks to the front to ask a girl something. Könecke continues teaching. *Oberschulrat* wanders slowly down the aisle, stops, looks out the window, stands a few minutes by his seat, and then sits down.
8:45	The three start talking about the class. Some children look over at them. They talk louder as Könecke writes on the board.
8:46	*Oberschulrat* gets up again, asks girl for her arithmetic notebook, sits down to look at it. Doering leans over to talk to him.
8:48	*Oberschulrat* gives notebook back to girl.
8:50	Doering says something to *Oberschulrat.*
8:53	*Oberschulrat* gets up again and wanders around, looks at pictures on the wall, then stands in middle of aisle and watches Könecke teach. *Oberschulrat* walks down toward the front, crosses between Könecke and students, and comes back to seat.
8:58	The three are talking again, in voices loud enough to bring glances from students.

9:00   Könecke asks student in front something. Student answers rather softly. *Oberschulrat* says sharply from back, *"Laut, laut"* [loud, loud].

9:01   Doering speaks to *Oberschulrat*.

9:02   Könecke studies his teaching plan before continuing.

9:03   Könecke tells students to get out arithmetic text. *Obserschulrat* gets up and goes to student to look at one.

9:04   *Oberschulrat* wanders down the aisle. With his foot he nudges feet of student which aren't directly under the student. Tells him to straighten up and use good posture. Tells another the same. Könecke goes on teaching. *Oberschulrat* tells another student to use blotter when writing.

9:06   Könecke asks girl a question. She starts to stand up. *Obserschulrat* says, "Sit down; you don't have to stand up during arithmetic."

9:08   Confusion about the books. Könecke has been using one book and the students have another so he has to write the problem on the board. A tense moment. Könecke starts to write. *Oberschulrat* says sharply, "Abbreviate so that the kids can get to work on the problem." *Oberschulrat* tells Könecke some words he can abbreviate.

9:09   *Oberschulrat* talks rather loudly with other two in back.

9:12   *Oberschulrat* gets up and opens window. Doering also opens one.

9:13   *Oberschulrat* starts down the aisle again. Corrects a girl's arithmetic along the way. Stands at board by Könecke. A student answers a question using DM. *Oberschulrat* shakes his head in disgust and says, "You still say DM in the village; you should simply say Mark and write DM."

9:14   *Oberschulrat* walks back up the aisle and talks to Doering. Complains about warm room. Doering opens more windows.

9:15   *Oberschulrat* looks at another notebook as Könecke goes to another problem.

9:16   All three are writing.

9:20   Doering leans back to tell *Oberschulrat* something; the three talk.

9:23   Könecke begins to sum up.

9:25   *Oberschulrat* says something to Doering and then gets up and goes to front and tells Könecke he will take over. There are history dates on the board that the seventh grade teacher has put there. *Oberschulrat* asks students about them.

9:30   *Oberschulrat* excuses Könecke and tells kids to leave the room for recess.

Of all the activities, problems, and interpersonal relations I observed in the school the events of that morning incorporated most dramatically the forces and cultural directives that create the pressures and constraints characteristic of school life. The *Oberschulrat* was in his early sixties and close to retirement age. He was by reputation and demeanor a crusty, demanding person, who exploited all the authority and prestige of his office—the true embodiment of the stereotyped German bureaucrat. There was little disagreement among the teachers concerning their feelings about him. His presence on the school grounds, practically always unannounced, created an anxiety that permeated the atmosphere.

The teachers have encountered *Oberschulräte* who were more understanding and less imperious, but they have all been subjected to the same evaluation system, which is more overpowering than any single personality acting in an instrumental role. The *Oberschulrat* subjected Herr Könecke to the raw, almost merciless use of power; it was Herr Könecke's climatic experience with closure on his chosen profession. If one distills from these events the *Oberschulrat's* personality and mode of operation, there still remains a concentration of power, the dynamics of which, I am led to conclude, infuse the whole life of the school. It might be said that teachers really earn the job security they acquire with a successful completion of probation. But the psychological and cultural cost accounting required to protect an individual and an institution from the debilitating effects of such power must be measured in something other than mere financial units. The thrust of the power is never really blunted; it flows through the educational system and comes to rest in the classroom, where the student stands vulnerable, obligated to adjust to it, faced with no alternative.

Herr Könecke passed, but just barely. The judgment was that in all three classes he did not encourage the children to participate enough and did too much of the talking himself. His grade, Herr Doering felt, would make it difficult for him ever to become a principal, unless it were to happen late in his career. Furthermore, the chances of his locating a teaching position in Waldstadt (where he lived) were greatly damaged. What seemed to me to be especially tragic was that the whole matrix of power and human relationships provided little support for Herr Könecke in this crucial moment. As was his custom, he prepared thoroughly for the evaluation. His lesson plans (which he had to file with the county office) were worked out in minute detail, including the questions he intended to ask his pupils and the points at which he intended to ask them. But the authority exercised by the state in the system of teacher evaluation is decisive. The system at this point tends to isolate the candidate since there are few, if any, supportive forces at the local level. Teachers view this experience as a confrontation between the individual and the state. For Herr Könecke, it was a kind of isolation he could not afford.

THE FACULTY AND THE CHURCH

The first day of school begins in church. Before the first class, students report to the school grounds and move by classes down Herrenstrasse to the two churches, located three or four blocks apart. Regular worship services are held; the sermons usually concern the religious implications of a new school year.

In his comprehensive 1963 report to higher church authorities, Pfarrer Riedel of the Evangelical Church reported that in the past seven years no parent had refused religious instruction for his child, and no teacher had refused to give religious instruction. These conditions are characteristic of the church-school relationship. Religious instruction is mandatory, at least two to three hours each week in all elementary and secondary schools. The content of instruction is carefully outlined in the syllabus. The checks that the state exercises to insure conformity to the syllabus are imposed on religious instruction as well. The teacher is required to submit an outline covering the year's work, maintain the *Wochenbuch* [a weekly advance outline for each subject], and at the end of the year turn in a detailed report with titles of themes written and of songs and poems memorized.

The extent to which the church's presence pervades the life of the school and the community is no proof that this presence is not somewhat controversial—although less so in Rebhausen than other parts of the state. Two types of schools exist in the state, the *Christliche Gemeinschaft*—or *Simultanschule,* and the *Konfessionsschule.* The latter is found largely in areas which are predominantly Catholic. In the *Konfessionsschule,* religious instruction is given in only one denomination, either Protestant or Catholic. Parents who wish a different content in the instruction for their children must arrange a transfer to another community. The region in which Rebhausen is located has only *Simultan* schools, which is appropriate for Rebhausen with a church affiliation two-thirds Protestant and one-third Catholic. Under this arrangement, both affiliations have equal time in the schools.

Church control over the administration of religious instruction is considerable, based on a Concordat signed with the state. Teachers' performances in religious instruction are evaluated by church authorities. At least once every three years, both teachers and the clergy are observed in the classroom. In the lower grades the teachers generally teach religion; in the upper grades the clergy teach two of the three hours assigned to the subject. The responsibility is, among Rebhausen teachers, somewhat controversial. Teaching religion is not mandatory. A teacher can, when attending a teacher's college, exclude from his program the appropriate courses. But the pressures to take the normal route are considerable; refusal narrows job opportunities. Elementary school teachers are expected to teach all subjects, including religion. If they cannot, they are not as valuable to a school, and if the missing subject is religion, they are less acceptable to the community. All the Rebhausen teachers give religious instruction—some with little enthusiasm.

The church can expect from the Ministry of Education a balance of religious affiliations among faculty members that reflects the balance in the village. The church has also come to expect that the principal will always be of the same religious affiliation as the majority in the village. Herr Doering is Catholic and therefore a notable exception to this arrangement. When the position was vacated four years ago, Herr Doering decided, to the surprise of the community, to compete for it. He registered his intention with the county office.

Although the community has no control over teachers assigned to it, it does exercise some control over the selection of a principal. The county office sends the names of three candidates to the mayor who, along with the *Gemeinderat,* makes the selection. Herr Doering's name was among the three, and the debate was underway. He was a popular individual with teachers, parents, and local officials, but a Catholic in a predominantly Protestant village. The Evangelical Church Council, under the leadership of Pfarrer Riedel, supported his candidacy. There was, however, considerable opposition from church officials at the regional and state levels. They thought it a questionable exception to a workable arrangement. The wishes of the community prevailed and Herr Doering received the appointment—the best measure of the respect and affection he commands in Rebhausen.

Pfarrer Riedel and Pfarrer Kurtz are not only official members of the faculty but also channels of mediation between parents and the school, particularly with regard to issues involving religious instruction. Along with the principal and the mayor, they hear protests from parents who are either too shy to approach teachers directly or who want to build support for some change. Protests are minimal and usually involve an offense to the parent's religious belief system.

From the first day of the first grade, children experience the influence of the church on the life of the school and are constantly reminded of the religious division in the village. The schedule must be adjusted to this fact. When Evangelical children start the day with religious instruction, Catholic children come an hour later. When first graders are being accustomed to the schedule, there are almost daily announcements by teachers, such as "Evangelical children report tomorrow at 7:45 A.M.; Catholic children at 8:45." It is an administrative procedure that gives them an early lesson on the character of the community.

FACULTY AND PARENTS

Within the first few months of a new school year, each teacher is responsible for calling a meeting of parents and seeing that two representatives to the parents' council are elected. When the process is completed, the principal calls a meeting of the council to elect officers and to consider the role of the council and the needs of the school. Rektor Doering convened the meeting in early June; Herr Bergmann, the bank president, was re-elected president and Herr Schroder, the town clerk, re-elected vice-president. No vote was taken; by informal acclamation the group was happy to have the two men continue in their offices.

Herr Bergmann, representing the council to the principal, reiterated his statement of graduation night that the function of the council is to intervene in the affairs of the school when a problem that requires outside mediation arises between parents and school personnel. He considered the leadership of the school to be in excellent hands and the faculty to be competent. There was, therefore, no need for the council to be active. Herr Doering acquiesced and suggested that members of the council could help the school by bringing parental complaints to him.

The narrow interpretation of the council's interests reflect certain historical and social developments. The council itself is new to the life of the village, a product of a constitutional promulgation following World War II. Second, the traditional social structure of the village has dictated a distinct social distance between teachers and parents. Teachers, along with the mayor and clergy, have occupied the apex in village society. They are *Respektpersonen,* a classification which assigns to them the whole catalog of social amenities the traditional culture has created for ranking members. Since the determination of educational policies and directives is the domain of the state, the operating space of such a council is narrowly constrained.

Third, parents are also generally satisfied with the relationships between teachers and pupils. Most parents experienced a more severe discipline in their school days than that to which their children are exposed. What they observe now is a more comradely relationship, a development they welcome, at least as it manifests itself in the immediate, daily life of the school. However, the trend is also suggestive of a weakening in the discipline and order of the traditional folk life. When parents observe that the children no longer always give teachers their due respect (such as crossing the street to greet them), they feel a tinge of regret. A few parents view this "degeneration" with disgust.

A final factor is the attitude of the faculty. They view the council with mixed emotions. A friendly, cooperative relationship with parents is considered desirable. At the same time, the whole matrix of relationships is, teachers know, relatively unexplored and therefore unpredictable. They suspect that the council, as an institution, might lead to a habit of parental intervention which, unrestrained, could challenge the professional and personal authority of the teacher. The only control device available to them is a kind of cautious indifference. They prefer to organize the one parent meeting required of them and call additional meetings only when parents are needed to act on a problem the teachers want to solve. The uncertainty of teachers about the council is aggravated by the growing presence of a constituency over which they exercise less influence. Factory parents are not integrated into the life of the community and are not, therefore, subject to the traditional constraints which the folk culture imposes. For them, in this setting at least, teachers are not necessarily *Respektpersonen*.

Confronting the centers of power and prestige in the community, of which the school is one, is for the average Rebhausen native an unwieldy experience. Consequently, when an excited parent shows up at the school to lodge a complaint or submit the same in writing, the whole process is characterized by an awkward, brittle, unpredictable quality. By general understanding, parents are to seek out the teacher during the school day, at any one of the recesses. There are no conference periods set up after school, when a parent can talk quietly and privately. Sometimes this kind of exchange takes place, but it is generally accidental and does not usually involve a redress of grievances. Parents locate a teacher and have five minutes to reach an understanding, while they stand outside the classroom with students milling about as the recess begins and ends. Whatever sense of urgency the parent comes with is usually compounded by conditions forcing a hurried, excited exchange.

On a morning late in February, two parents appeared at the school with particularly vehement protests about low grades their children had received and disciplinary action they had experienced. The mother and grandfather who accosted Frau Schenke became excited, almost abusive. Teachers crowded around to "protect" her. Herr Doering said afterward that, should this sort of thing happen again, he would ring the school bell three times, a signal for the teachers to gather. He thinks it important that the faculty present a united front in the face of criticism. Herr Doering and the faculty feel that this kind of parental behavior is more characteristic of rootless, working-class families attracted to Rebhausen by the factory. They are sure they have an understanding relationship with the natives.

The possible threat of legal action is often present in parent-teacher conflict.

Teachers are conscious enough of their legal vulnerability to feel, with some seriousness, that *"Ein Lehrer steht mit einen Fuss in einem Gefängnis,"* [A teacher stands with one foot in prison.] The teacher is, of course, responsible for whatever happens under his supervision, on the school grounds, in the classroom, on a field trip. The kind of incident that can produce legal action was described to me by one of the teachers. A child bumped her head in the classroom, at a time when the teacher had stepped out of the room to speak to a parent. The supervision was not there; the child had headaches for a week following the incident. A suit did not develop only because the faculty was able to persuade the parents not to file one.

Certain legal cases in the state have had such disastrous results for the teachers involved that much has been published by educational organizations to remind teachers of the precautions they should take. The norms for the use of corporal punishment that teachers are expected to follow and that reflect state policy can be summarized as follows:

1. Corporal punishment of girls and of children in the first and second grades is forbidden.
2. In the education of boys, corporal punishment is to be eliminated. It is permitted to be used only in very rare cases.
3. Teachers still on probation are absolutely forbidden to use corporal punishment.
4. In each school there is to be a punishment log or record set up and each act of corporal punishment entered, with a short explanation for its necessity.
5. The teacher must understand that it is a denial of his dignity when he uses corporal punishment.
6. If it must be done, use a stick on the rear end—nothing else.
7. The best advice is just do not use corporal punishment.

The policy of the state is in obvious conflict with the practice of corporal punishment in the Rebhausen school. It is clear that, despite the power the Ministry of Education exercises over the professional advancement of teachers, the latter do not accept the policy as binding, and state authorities do not choose to enforce the policy. They appear willing to wait until legal action, instituted by a parent, forces state intervention. This ambiguity leaves Rebhausen teachers uncertain as to the course such intervention will take. Consequently they are beginning to be more cautious in their use of physical punishment. They agree that native parents consider a teacher weak if he does not use force when appropriate, but that factory parents will be more likely to intervene on behalf of the child when force is used. They conclude it behooves a teacher to know the parent whose child he is about to punish.

THE PRINCIPAL AND THE MAYOR

The relationship between the school and local government depends on the personalities of the two major protagonists, the mayor and the principal, and on the tenacity and specificity with which the mayor carries out his responsibilities. The principal possesses no administrative interest in village government. His domain of authority is limited to the school. However, although faculty salaries are paid by the state, the construction, furnishing, and repair of school buildings are financial obligations of the village, along with the cost of textbooks and other instructional materials. In addition, because the mayor is involved in the selection of the principal, he has a definite administrative interest in the educational system.

The mayor and Herr Doering have a common commitment to help the community and the school adjust to and participate constructively in the urban, industrial culture, which is spreading out from the population centers and engulfing the folk life of their village. They are both deeply and energetically involved in implementing this commitment: the mayor with his long range plan for the expansion of community facilities, and Herr Doering with his interests in an orientation program, driver education, and English instruction. At the same time, their routine administrative duties tend to maintain separate spheres of action.

It is obvious the mayor has considerable respect for Herr Doering's ability as principal and his standing in the community. Otherwise, he would not have supported his appointment as principal. However, the mayor is moved periodically to remind the principal that he is the ranking official in the village. The pretense is usually an inspection of the school, a detail which is technically his responsibility but which he could leave to Herr Doering. When, for example, he showed up one winter day and expressed displeasure with the appearance of the hall (jackets piled high, general disarray), he was reminding Herr Doering of the relationship between the two. It is the kind of maneuver that might be expected where there exists areas of overlapping interests. The protocol traditional among village officials makes it inevitable that the resolution of such a conflict be affected through the blunt exercise of power.

THE FACULTY AS A GROUP

Rebhausen teachers are a friendly, open group of individuals. I spent hours with most of them discussing school life and related subjects, and visited them in their homes for long evenings of conversation and wine. I attended the coffee klatsch, a weekly gathering in the early afternoon of some of the younger teachers, and went bowling with them each month in a dilapidated, but *gemütlich,* old bowling alley in a nearby village.

Faculty interpersonal relationships are often delightfully informal. During "open house" at the new school building, while parents were inspecting and the older teachers were greeting them and answering questions, the younger teachers gathered in the faculty room. With the help of the janitor who located some wine, the cleaning lady who had brought some cake, and Herr Kost who had his guitar, the building got a real dedication.

Yet, however well they come to know each other, the formal social amenities so characteristic of village life are not ignored. Several of the younger women teachers, especially the two who room together use the informal *Du* with each other and first names. Most of the teachers use formal address and seldom if ever first names, regardless of age and standing. They always shake hands with each other in the morning and are careful to make certain they have not missed anyone, even if the process continues into the second or third period. The custom is warm and friendly, and when they are all together and about to depart—after a bowling evening for example—the handshaking tradition has all the complexities of an intricate dance routine.

The internal administration of the school creates no appreciable pressure for a teacher unless his performance is patently incompetent and disruptive of the school program. Teachers operate quite independently of the principal. The administrative decisions he has to make concerning such matters as teaching assignments and disciplinary cases among the students are accepted as integral to his position. When a case of dereliction of duty does occur, Herr Doering involves the faculty in the initiatory aspects of the process. During the year we were there a young man, assigned to the school as a physical education instructor on a part-time basis, was erratic in attendance and slipshod in supervising the children. He had been warned often by the principal without results, and because the end of the year was near, Herr Doering felt moved to take official action. He called the faculty together, in the faculty room during the fifteen-minute recess, and had, in Herr Volker's presence, charges of dereliction read and entered in the faculty log book. Herr Volker offered a few lame excuses, and the meeting was dismissed. Herr Doering said it was the first case he had ever carried so far. It meant, he said, that Herr Volker would not be assigned to Rebhausen the next year.

Most decisions over which the faculty holds autonomy are made democratically in faculty meetings. Under Herr Doering's leadership the group works well together. There are normal inter-personal strains, provoked, for example, by the distribution of teaching assignments or by conflicting points of view about appropriate classroom procedures. But the authority exercised by the Ministry of Education eliminates many potential sources of internal conflict.

FACULTY-STUDENT RELATIONS IN RETROSPECT

The methods of discipline used in the school have been described in detail. The attention given to this aspect of school life is not meant to suggest that it is the key to the character of Rebhausen life, but that it is certainly basic to assessing the forceful, definitive enculturation process, which the school structures. Within the framework of the total disciplinary pattern and the general tenor of teacher-student relationships, the specific kind of punishment utilized has less significance. It is one strand in an intricately woven fabric.

Most elements in the teacher-pupil exchange establish and reinforce an unbending relationship, in which the pupil learns to find the important cues to successful behavior and general school performance in the teacher's words and actions. The content of the student's learning experiences is almost awlays rigidly controlled by the teacher. Opportunities for manifesting and expressing individualistic renditions of this content are constrained within narrow limits. The recitation process is, in this respect, particularly significant. Lines of communication run almost exclusively between individual students and the teacher, with the latter controlling and directing the content of the communication. Only in a few instances does any meaningful exchange occur, in which students examine each other's ideas. In one sense students are, in the classroom, isolated from each other intellectually and therefore more vulnerable to and dependent on the dictates of the teacher.

The almost limitless power of the teacher seems to affect the kind of respect he displays toward students. One has the feeling that the respect must be earned either through academic performance or through appropriate behavior. There is little psychological protection in the classroom for those who have difficulty measuring up to acceptable standards. Their exposure is constant, with few avenues of relief available.

The more informal teacher-student contacts during the school day tend to reinforce the dominant relationship. Any relaxed interchange, before or after class, about the academic content is almost totally absent. Teachers prefer to gather together, smoke, and talk during the recesses. Pupils grow up learning to be ready to perform personal favors for the teachers during these free minutes. They may be asked to buy cigarettes across the street at the drugstore, hurry to the bakery for a teacher's mid-morning snack, get a quart of milk at the dairy, or carry the teacher's briefcase to the classroom when he arrives in the building. They do these things gladly and cheerfully (at least the younger children). The errands present an excuse to leave the building or the playground and are certainly far less onerous than pruning tomato plants or feeding the pigs—which was what their parents sometimes had to do in an era when limited finances forced teachers to engage in such enterprises.

When teachers and students are together there is seldom any release from this highly directive, intense relationship. When the setting is the countryside during a hike or the dormitory at a youth hostel, instead of the school building, the teacher as chaperone has to exercise careful direction of student activities. In spite of such constraints, these shared experiences are meaningful for both teachers and students. It seems that what is required, to affect some kind of release is a third, mediating influence—nature or song.

The mayor had told the eighth graders that he always hoped the village would elect *anständige Leute* to the *Gemeinderat.* During interviews teachers consistently identified *anständig* as the personal trait they considered most important for students to develop. Basically the word means *decent* and *respectable,* but it is undoubtedly invested with cultural significance that can never be completely delineated. In Rebhausen, when parents and teacher admonished children to be *anständig,* I understood them to be demanding behavior that displays in interpersonal relations a respect for traditional social amenities and distinctions and that reflects positively on home and school.

The importance to teachers of this behavior cannot be explained simply in terms

of the norms of village life. It has been the purpose of
broader setting in which to place school life, particularly (
ers. This setting illustrates the importance in a folk cultur
ship between the village and the urban environment.
such a relationship with institutions and power centers outsi(
also accumulate valuable evidence concerning the cultural (
plement and the set toward students that is most appropriate

It is clear that Rebhausen teachers themselves experience
operation of the state school system an authority comparabl
ercise in the classroom. However well-established a teacher
senzimmer, the state Ministry of Education is the real king. The
to a teacher in an isolated village through a well-organized bureaucra
which each level is invested with ample power to act effectively towaru
subordinate level. Furthermore, the culture of this bureaucracy appears to lack
ioning attributes—in terms of interpersonal relations—which render a subordinat
position more tolerable. Thus it is fair to say that the kind of respect Rebhausen
teachers show students is in part the result of the kind of respect shown them by
their superiors.

Chapter 6, the concluding chapter, begins with a vignette of village life, a dedication ceremony. The ceremony took place only a week before we left Rebhausen so
it had a sense of climax for us as well as the residents. Its significance lies, however, in what it emphasizes about the conditions and problems of tradition and
change in Rebhausen.

6 / Conclusions: a perspective on tradition and change

I

N THE SUMMER of 1965 Rebhausen celebrated the dedication of a new school. It is a modern structure—spacious, handsomely furnished, located on a knoll overlooking the center of town, and flanked by gardens and grape terraces. The building had been in use since the beginning of the new school year in the spring; it had been impossible to wait until the completion of construction. The old structure, built in 1903, was woefully inadequate for the school population: when the four upper grades moved into the new building, all classrooms in both buildings were occupied. In the aura of pride and good feelings that surrounded the dedication—and considering the cost and indebtedness the village had incurred— the crowded conditions were not a welcome subject for discussion. But teachers in particular were aware that the projected population growth was underestimated. Realistically speaking, Rebhausen had to begin immediately to plan for an expansion of the new structure. The miscalculation was indicative of the accelerated change the village was experiencing and of the inadequate comprehension of village leadership about the implications of such change.

Nevertheless, the dedication ceremony renewed, in the midst of change, a sense of the past and reaffirmed for natives the validity of the traditional and enduring school life. Children from all classes participated in a humorous skit about schools. The children's choir sang; music for guitar and recorder was played; poems were recited. In all the dramatic renditions, expression was forceful and appropriate and memorization almost flawless.

Adults performed well too. The men's choir, the village band, and fife-and-drum corp were on the program. One or more of these groups are practically always present to perform on any festive occasion, such as a dedication ceremony, an annual meeting, an anniversary celebration of some club, or even the birthday of an elderly native. (When a person reaches seventy-five, the mayor arranges to have one of the musical organizations play or sing at every birthday thereafter.) The average age of the band and the fife-and-drum corp is less than that of the men's choir. These two groups include several talented *Volksschule* students, and because they are both marching groups, they are more festive and lively in their performances. The men's choir, in contrast, is sedate and solemn in its public appearances. The oldest organization in the village, it is also the most prestigious. The membership includes venerable Rebhausen citizens. Leadership roles are assigned according to standing in the village as well as activity in the organization; elections are at times more heated and provoke more interest than village elections. The organization's repertoire is varied but includes for almost every occasion sentimental renditions of *Heimatlieder* [songs of the homeland].

So Rebhausen natives performed at the dedication ceremony. The musical talents that had been nurtured in the school were being displayed there once more by fathers, uncles, grandfathers, older cousins, and family acquaintances of the schoolchildren. Factory personnel were not represented in the organizations, but they were, as parents, in attendance at the dedication. For them the ceremony was not and could not be renewal. It was rather a celebration of change and progress, and the new building was impressive evidence of what the factory was doing to change the façade of village life. At the end of the ceremony, *wurst* and rolls were dis-

The new school.

tributed to the children, a tradition which grandparents in the audience had enjoyed as children when the old school building was dedicated in 1903.

When classes began in the new building, some Rebhausen children experienced change not only in the physical surroundings but also in the content of their instruction. Throughout West Germany a potentially far-reaching school reform program is underway, spurred by the recognition that the nation has been abysmally negligent of education for a technological age. The reform program is directed in particular at affecting changes in the structure, organization, and internal articulation of the elementary and secondary school system. The purpose is to wrench the system free of its rigid, elite-oriented character and to evolve a more flexible, open-class sytem.

Rebhausen children, in the year we were there, began to experience the benefits of the school reform movement. The organization of homogeneous grouping in several subjects in the fifth and sixth grades was a change instituted in the spring of 1965. The statewide goal is a more effective and exhaustive effort at identifying capable students—particularly in rural areas where such talent has been traditional-ly ignored or misplaced. The content of the program is aimed at making it possible for elementary school children to move into nonvocational schools at levels beyond the customary fourth and fifth grades. Since, in nonvocational schools, foreign lan-guage instruction begins with the fifth grade, including foreign language instruc-tion in the elementary school curriculum is necessary to enable students to move more freely between one type of school and another. Consequently, in April 1965, ap-proximately half of the Rebhausen fifth and sixth graders began the study of English.

Another basic change that will affect Rebhausen children is the addition of a ninth school year. It has long been argued at the state and national levels that eight years of compulsory school is inadequate to the needs of the nation. Some states and cities, especially in the north, have already implemented both a ninth and tenth year. By 1970 all schools in the state are to have the ninth year. The curriculum is to include considerable emphasis on civic-political education in a modern world.

The reaction of Rebhausen natives to these changes is mixed. For the full-time farmer, faced with a critical labor shortage, the ninth year is a needless repetition of what students have already learned. He wants his boy through school and on the farm as soon as possible. Along with many other natives he sees practically no value in the ninth year for girls. One more year in school means one less year of work before marriage.

But changes in Rebhausen are working to diminish the influence of full-time farming as the primary economic activity and central, cohesive theme in the life of the village. Primitive farming methods and a subsistence standard of living had through the years structured shared patterns of work and unifying modes of social interaction. The struggle to extract a living from the soil was a common struggle. The resources of whole neighborhoods were pooled in moments of emergency, such as sickness, accidents, a breakdown in equipment, or peak work periods. Families and neighbors evolved informal but effective patterns of reciprocal help. At night in the winter, families took turns entertaining their neighbors. The occasion was quiet, restful talk; the purpose was to save electricity. Few families could afford to burn their lights every night.

Flurbereinigung, mechanization, state regulation, the factory, and full employ-ment in an expanding economy are factors creating new work patterns and chang-ing modes of social interaction. The use of tractors and other motorized equipment in fields that have been consolidated is reducing man-hour requirements and mak-ing the full- or part-time farmer less dependent on manual labor. The state regula-tions prohibiting the uneconomic division of farm property among siblings has elim-inated the *Erbteilung,* a tradition that in a positive sense helped bind the extended family together, but in a negative sense, frustrated nonagricultural vocational aspi-rations. In the midst of these changes the factory suddenly appeared and thrust into village life its insatiable demand for workers. But, if a young or marginal farmer does not find work there appealing, he can choose among jobs in the next village or in the city.

By their own standards, Rebhausen natives are more prosperous than they have ever been before. But the cost of living is high and they do not trust the prosperity, so their pace is feverish. Two jobs are better than one—shift work in the factory and part-time *Weinbau,* the latter a profitable operation and, more important, the embodiment of economic security and cultural continuity.

The village treasurer had said that Rebhausen is becoming more impersonal. Most natives share this feeling. Farm operations are performed more independently. Shift work in the factory is a relatively impersonal social experience. A rising standard of living is making possible the increased purchase of cars, which makes available new forms of recreation outside the village. A Sunday walk and visit had been and still is traditional in Rebhausen. But, as one native remarked, "You can't count on people's being home now that so many own cars."

Natives and factory families have not yet found or evolved many avenues of social interaction with each other. Nevertheless, the factory families constitute a social presence that is beginning to exercise an influence on the native population, particularly on the vocational aspirations native parents hold for their children. Teachers continually assert that factory children are no smarter than native children, but the feeling is common that the performance of the former is superior. Almost all children in Rebhausen who commute each day to Waldstadt *Gymnasien* are factory children. Parents listen to tales their own children bring home from school and are aware that the factory children are already better equipped to confront the changing, moving, urban world of industry.

There is among native parents, however, little discontent with the school. This is less true of factory families; a small number of parents, who intend for their children to be admitted to a *Gymnasium* at the end of the fourth grade, express some dissatisfaction with the lack of adequate preparation for the *Gymnasium.* Personal grievances about grades, discipline, or the inconveniences of the schedule develop among the natives from time to time. But they are isolated instances and reflect no growing body of opinion about the inadequacies of the school program. The socialization process that children experience in the school constitutes no marked deviation from family patterns of child rearing. The use of physical punishment, shame, and peer censorship to affect acceptable patterns of behavior in the schools reflects social devices that parents use and that they themselves experienced in school. The fact that most parents welcome the freer, more informal relationship developing between teachers and children is a reflection both of a negative reaction to the severe socialization parents themselves experienced and of a general but slow relaxation of restraints in a democratic-industrial society.

The administration of the academic content to which Rebhausen children are exposed represents no radical departure from that which parents had experienced. Some parents wonder hesitantly if it is really necessary for their children to memorize so many historical facts in an age that is rapidly changing. But this is a passing question. The primary emphasis on arithmetic and German is from a parental standpoint appropriate and functional. The skillful attention teachers give to literature, poetry, drama, and music proves instrumental in passing on to children those overt expressions of the culture with which parents are familiar and which are important channels of friendly, meaningful social interaction, and cultural reaffirmation.

Had there existed among parents deeply felt discontentment, few social devices can be utilized for coalescing such feelings into effective pressures for change. While school children are enjoying a more informal relationship with teachers, parents have experienced a pronounced social distance. The Parent Council, a post-war addition to village life, therefore remains a formality with little operational relationship to the school. It is seen as an institution concerned primarily with mediating sharp grievances between parents and teachers. Consequently, it has as yet no continuing utility, whereby parents can begin to experience a closer relationship to the school and to learn the art of affecting informal social action and pressure. Village life in general provides Rebhausen natives few institutions in which discontentment can be informally confronted. Grievances among neighbors, for example, are adjudicated by the mayor, as grievances among children are settled by the teacher. Finally, the fact that teachers are employees of the state rather than of the community serves to protect the school from parents and to discourage the latter from developing a sense of vested interest in the life of the school.

Like the factory personnel the teachers as a group are oriented toward the life of the city. Their interests and outlook are cosmopolitan; they are well educated, well read and well traveled. Two of them live in Waldstadt and drive ten miles each day to Rebhausen. Unlike the factory personnel, however, the teachers are not strangers to the village. The social structure of Rebhausen provides immediate entrance for teachers, as *Respektpersonen* occupying a prestige position. A teacher may eventually win the affection of natives through his personality, behavior, and teaching style, but informal social interaction does not increase at the same rate. In spite of their nonrural interests, teachers belong to the life of the village; they represent no threat to the integrity of village life and mores. On the contrary, parents tend to see teachers as allies in the struggle to protect the traditional processes of socialization from nefarious urban influences. Such influences threaten the traditional authority of both the teacher and the parent.

Teachers are at work in modest ways helping students become better acquainted with the characteristics and demands of an urban-industrial way of life. (The principal's eighth grade orientation program is an example.) But, as employees of the state, teachers are inclined with good reason to operate within the confines of state policy, as it is directly pronounced and implemented or inferred from past action. Because there is, inevitably perhaps, a bureaucratic no man's land where teachers are not sure of the limits on innovation, they tend to be conservative, and the local culture reinforces this conservatism. The teaching style which most effectively sustains the prestige and authority of the teacher reflects socialization values characteristic of Rebhausen family life. Consequently the faculty constitutes a force for stability in the midst of change, and the school functions primarily as a transmitter of the traditional culture.

Recommended Reading

FOSTER, GEORGE M., 1953, "What is Folk Culture?", *American Anthropologist*, 55:159–73.

A valuable discussion of folk culture and its relationship to nonfolk cultures.

FRIEDL, ERNESTINE, 1962, *Vasilika, A Village in Modern Greece*. New York: Holt, Rinehart and Winston, Inc.

In a study of a Greek village, the author found that the school system played a vital role in cultural maintenance, particularly with regard to the reinforcement of family mores and value commitments.

KOB, JANPETER, 1963, *Erziehung in Elternhaus und Schule*. Stuttgart, West Germany: Ferdinand Enke Verlag.

A sociological study of interrelationships among parents, pupils and teachers with respect to attitudes toward school life, aspirations and other aspects of education. Attention is given to rising expectations in an increasingly industrial society.

MUTH, JAKOB, 1963, *Das ende der Volksschule*. Essen, West Germany: Neue Deutsche Schule Verlagsgesellschaft.

A consideration of the evolving role and function of the elementary school in German society.

PICHT, GEORG, 1964, *Die Deutsche Bildungskatastrophe*. Freiburg, West Germany: Walter Verlag.

A general polemic about the state of German education with particular attention to conditions leading to a shortage of Gymnasium and university graduates and of teachers. The book has been a major contribution in stimulating debate about educational issues.

SCHNEIDER, FRIEDRICH, 1957, *Die Dorfschule*. Münich, West Germany: Bayerischer Landwirtschaftsverlag.

An analysis of the German rural school in the light of expanding urban influences. Consideration is given to the curriculum, rural in its orientation, but which now must serve a population increasingly urban in its orientation.

SPINDLER, GEORGE D., 1963, *Education and Culture*. New York: Holt, Rinehart and Winston, Inc.

A variety of reactions to the prospect or threat of cultural change is possible. Articles by the editor and other contributors are especially directed toward the analysis of the processes of adaptation to social, economic, and cultural change characterizing schools in different societies.

VIDICH, ARTHUR and JOSEPH BENSMAN, 1958, *Small Town in Mass Society*. New York: Doubleday & Company, Inc.

In their treatment of the schools, the authors show that the more formal, structured elements in a school culture may acquire significance beyond their original purpose.

WURZBACHER, GERHARD, 1961, *Das Dorf im Spannungsfeld Industrieller Entwicklung.* Stuttgart, West Germany: Ferdinand Enke Verlag.

This research on West German communities points to a transition in social controls as a result of the increased freedom of the individual from traditional family and neighborhood controls.

WYLIE, LAURENCE, 1961, *Village in the Vaucluse.* Cambridge, Mass.: Harvard University Press.

The significance of the educational system is given careful attention in this study of a French community. The author found that the patterning of behavior in the schools was more a reflection of the total culture than it was simply of the operational objectives of the schools themselves.